MW01488377

One Minute Devos

A Place at His Table

365 One Minute Devotions

Roy Lessin

A Place at His Table: 365 One Minute Devotions

First Edition, December 2019

Published by:

P.O. Box 1010
Siloam Springs, AR 72761
dayspring.com

Printed in China
Prime: J1596
ISBN: 978-1-64454-445-7

January 1

The Shepherd *of the* Meadow

"But his bow remained firm and steady
[in the Strength that does not fail],
For his arms were made strong and agile
By the hands of the Mighty One of Jacob,
(By the name of the Shepherd, the Stone of Israel).

GENESIS 49:24 AMP

The Lord is not only your Good Shepherd who leads you to the meadow of grace, but He is every provision you will find in the meadow—He is the green pastures you rest in; He is the quiet waters you drink from; He is the restoration of your soul; He is the way that keeps your feet on righteous paths; He is your victory over the powers of death and evil; He is the rod and staff of your covering and comfort; He is the banquet your hungry soul feasts upon; He is the goodness and the lovingkindness that is yours forever.

JANUARY 2

THE LORD IS YOUR ALL

The LORD is my…
PSALM 23:1 KJV

The Lord: Yahweh. The Eternal. Jehovah. I Am. The self-existent One. The God of forever and ever.

is: Not will be one day. Not someday. Not was a long time ago. Is now, at this very moment—as I draw each breath, as I take each step, as I face each circumstance of life.

my: Not just someone else's. Not just the pastor's. Not just the missionary's. Not just the people in the Bible. Personal God. My God. Knowing me intimately, watching me carefully, loving me fully.

January 3

You're *in the* Good Shepherd's Care

The Lord is my shepherd…

PSALM 23:1 KJV

Shepherd: Pastor. The One who tends, keeps, guards, guides. The Good Shepherd; the Great Shepherd; the Chief Shepherd. The One who leads. The One who feeds. Life giver. Care giver. Watching every moment; protecting in every situation; providing every need. Laying down His life. Giving His all. Seeking me. Carrying me. Holding me close.

January 4

The Lord Is Your Provider

The Lord is my shepherd; I shall not want.
PSALM 23:1 KJV

I: His hand is on me. I am the apple of His eye. I am His beloved. I am His child. I am His possession. I belong to Him. I am in His hands. I am in His thoughts. I am on His heart.

shall not: Never! Not once! Not in any circumstance; not in any trial; not at any age. I am certain, sure, persuaded, unmistaken, absolutely confident of His "yes" to me.

want: He is my supply. He is my provider. He is my provision. I shall not be given a stone instead of bread. I shall not come up empty, be destitute, find out that I have been forsaken. In Him, my Lord, my God, my Shepherd, my Pastor, I find no lack.

January 5

He Knows How *to* Look after You

The Lord is my shepherd; I shall not want. He maketh me...

Psalm 23:1–2 KJV

He: Not fate. Not "the gods." Not luck. Not self-help. Not philosophy. He alone! Creator God. Father, Son, Holy Spirit. Maker of all things. Keeper of all things. Ruler of all things in heaven, in earth, in my life.

maketh: Not wishful thinking, not pie-in-the-sky, but reality. He makes the way and gives the opportunity. He leads me to His prepared place. He makes it possible in every circumstance. He lets me; He insists upon it—I do not need to question or wonder what His will is in the matter.

me: Personal God! He understands my particular needs and knows where and how to look after me. His gaze is on me. His care is upon me. His love is over me.

January 6

He Is Your Rest

The Lord is my shepherd; I shall not want. He maketh me to lie down in green pastures...

PSALM 23:1–2 KJV

To lie down: Legs folded, knees bent. No striving. No panic. No running about in haste or going around in circles. A time to stop, to kneel, to bend. Reclining—no "standing up" on the inside in protest or rebellion.

in: Not in imagination. Not in fantasy. Not in pretend or make believe. In truth. In my heart, in my soul, in my spirit. In Him—the Way, the Truth, the Life.

green pastures: His tender, caring place. Luscious. Satisfying. Nurturing. Sustaining. Refreshing. Delighting. Pastures free of dryness, emptiness, barrenness, hopelessness, despair, confusion, death.

January 7

He Leads You *in* Footsteps *of* Grace

The Lord is my shepherd; I shall not want. He maketh me to lie down in green pastures. He leadeth me...

PSALM 23:1-2 KJV

He: Not governments. Not politicians. Not political parties. Not programs. Not schemes and the plans of men. He alone! Mighty God, ruler of the land and sea. Giver and sustainer of my life—my glory and the lifter of my head.

leadeth me: Not pushing. Not driving. Not far removed, but ever-present, ever-near. Out front. Taking the first steps, going before, making the pathway passable, possible, doable with footsteps of grace.

January 8

His Place *for* You Is Peace

The Lord is my shepherd; I shall not want.
He maketh me to lie down in green pastures:
He leadeth me beside the still waters.
Psalm 23:1–2 KJV

Beside: Not looking at His provisions from a distance. Not far off. Not held at a distance. Not watching someone else enjoy His blessings while I am asked to take a step back or step aside. Close. Near. Placing me right where I need to be…right where He is.

the still waters: Not babbling brooks, not shooting rapids, but peaceful pools. No turmoil. Not a place to rile up but a place to calm down. A still place, a quiet place, a restful place. To be as still as He is, because He gives His peace. Here I leave everything in His care and His keeping…letting go so He can hold all. My heart is quiet, my soul is still.

January 9

Your Life Is *in* His Hands

The Lord is my shepherd; I shall not want. He maketh me to lie down in green pastures: He leadeth me beside the still waters. He restoreth…

PSALM 23:1–3 KJV

He: The God of all grace and tender mercies. The God of healing rain. Great Physician—whose healing balm mends my wounds, soothes my pains, comforts my troubled heart. God of the welcoming voice, the gentle way, the reassuring touch.

restoreth: Not neglecting. Not ignoring. Not denying. Assuring me "He can" and "He will." Lifting me when I am down; carrying me when I have fallen; refreshing me when I am stale; renewing me when I am weary; turning my head when I have become distracted; rescuing me when I am in danger; pulling me back when I am drifting away. Molding and shaping my clay within His masterful hands to conform me to His image. Making all things new.

January 10

He Knows You Best

The Lord is my shepherd; I shall not want. He maketh me to lie down in green pastures: He leadeth me beside the still waters. He restoreth my soul…

PSALM 23:1–3 KJV

My soul: Who I am in reality. My personality in all its complexity. My mind—thoughts and plans, what I think upon, what I dwell upon. My emotions—feelings, moods, highs and lows. My will—choices, decisions, what I determine to do, where I determine to go. My appetites. My longings. His grace causing me to think His thoughts, feel what He feels, choose what He chooses. Bringing within me the times of refreshing that come from the presence of the Lord.

January 11

Guided *in* Wisdom, Kept *by* Love

The Lord is my shepherd; I shall not want.
He maketh me to lie down in green pastures:
He leadeth me beside the still waters. He
restoreth my soul: He leadeth me…

PSALM 23:1–3 KJV

He: Not astrology. Not philosophy. My God, my Guide, my Guardian. He from whom are all things, by whom are all things, through whom are all things. He in whom I live, and move, and have my being. The only true time traveler.

leadeth me: Not pointlessly. Not wrongfully. Not mischievously. Not aimlessly. Knowing what He is doing. Knowing where He is going. Knowing what is best. Showing the way, making the way, providing the way, being the way. Bestowing the blessings that make me rich; bringing the joys that make me full; imparting the strength that makes me able to follow His footsteps.

January 12

All His Plans Are Good *and* Right

The Lord is my shepherd; I shall not want. He maketh me to lie down in green pastures: He leadeth me beside the still waters. He restoreth my soul: He leadeth me in the paths of righteousness...

PSALM 23:1–3 KJV

In the paths of righteousness: Not vanity. Not sin. Not selfishness. Making straight paths for my feet—not the path of self-effort, not the path of self-righteousness, not the path of dead works. A path of mercy. A path of faith. A path of rest. A path that keeps me from regrets. Freeing me from restlessness and anxiousness; from the hurts and disappointments of life; from the worries and fears that want to cast their shadow upon the course He has chosen for me to follow. A beautiful path. A peaceful path. A joy-filled path that leads me straight to His heart.

January 13

To Know Him Is *to* Know *the* Best

The Lord is my shepherd; I shall not want.
He maketh me to lie down in green pastures:
He leadeth me beside the still waters. He
restoreth my soul: He leadeth me in the paths
of righteousness for His name's sake.

PSALM 23:1–3 KJV

For His name's sake: Not for my applause, recognition, or celebration. Not my light but His glory. Not my reputation but His honor. Not my cleverness but His majesty. Holy One. Mighty One. Wondrous One. Awesome One. Amazing God. Name above all names. King above all kings. Lord above all lords. Transcendent. Immutable. Worthy to receive all the praise and thanks my heart can give.

January 14

The One Who Leads You Is Wonderful

The Lord is my shepherd; I shall not want. He maketh me to lie down in green pastures: He leadeth me beside the still waters. He restoreth my soul: He leadeth me in the paths of righteousness for His name's sake. Yea, though I walk…

PSALM 23:1–4 KJV

Yea: Yes to You, Jesus. Yes to Your will, Your way, Your plan, Your purpose. Yes to what seems possible and impossible. Yes to what You have prepared, to where Your footsteps are going—through places unknown, to destinations unimagined, by pathways never taken before.

though I walk: Not in panic, not in haste, not in perplexity. Walking, not running ahead. Walking, not dragging behind. Walking forward, not backward. Going at His pace. Planting my feet in His freshest footprints. Not getting stuck. Not standing in place. Pressing on.

January 15

He Is with You *in the* Difficult Place

The Lord is my shepherd; I shall not want.
He maketh me to lie down in green pastures:
He leadeth me beside the still waters. He
restoreth my soul: He leadeth me in the
paths of righteousness for His name's sake.
Yea, though I walk through the valley…

PSALM 23:1–4 KJV

Through the valley: Not always through the high places, not always through the mountaintops, not always through the grasslands, not always through the woodlands, not always through the bright and brilliant flowering fields and open skies of blue. Not the place where the journey ends but where the journey takes on new depths and new meaning. The hidden place that presses me to His side, to His heartbeat, to His tender mercies.

January 16

He Will Never Let You Go

The Lord is my shepherd; I shall not want. He maketh me to lie down in green pastures: He leadeth me beside the still waters. He restoreth my soul: He leadeth me in the paths of righteousness for His name's sake. Yea, though I walk through the valley of the shadow of death...

PSALM 23:1–4 KJV

Of the shadow of death: Tears. Sorrow. Trials and testing. The place where seeds of desires fall into the ground. The place where I let go, surrender all, declare from the depths of my being, "Not my will, but Thine, be done" (Luke 22:42 KJV). The place where I embrace His cross, am made conformable to His death, where I partake of the fellowship of His sufferings. The place where resurrection life overtakes me. The place where I feel His hand in mine—firm. Sure. Mighty. Never letting go.

January 17

He Frees You *from* Fear

The Lord is my shepherd; I shall not want. He maketh me to lie down in green pastures: He leadeth me beside the still waters. He restoreth my soul: He leadeth me in the paths of righteousness for His name's sake. Yea, though I walk through the valley of the shadow of death, I will fear no evil...

PSALM 23:1–4 KJV

I will fear no evil: The enemy, a defeated foe. His works destroyed by the power of Christ. Jesus my victor. Conquering King. Captain of my soul. Holy Spirit—Spirit, not of fear, but of power, love, and a sound mind. Heavenly Father—the One whom I have sought with all my heart; the One who hears and answers my prayer; the One who consistently, faithfully, triumphantly, delivers me from all my fears.

January 18

There's Never a Day *without* Him

The Lord is my shepherd; I shall not want. He maketh me to lie down in green pastures: He leadeth me beside the still waters. He restoreth my soul: He leadeth me in the paths of righteousness for His name's sake. Yea, though I walk through the valley of the shadow of death, I will fear no evil: for Thou art with me...

PSALM 23:1–4 KJV

For Thou art with me: There can be nothing sweeter, nearer, dearer than this—"Thou," Creator God, lover of my soul—with me, near me, by me, for me, in me. Fullness of joy! Pleasures forevermore! Not playing hide-and-seek with my soul, my heart, or my very being. Ever present help in time of need.

January 19

Your Father Makes No Mistakes

Yea, though I walk through the valley of the shadow of death, I will fear no evil: for Thou art with me; Thy rod and Thy staff they comfort me.

PSALM 23:4 KJV

Thy rod and Thy staff: The things You use to reach me, teach me, shape me, direct me, assure me, protect me. The rod of correction that never harms. The staff that pulls me close when I wander, that rescues me from the pit when I fall. Letting nothing slip by. Doing everything in love and for love's sake.

they comfort me: Not frustrated. Not bullied. Not stressed. Not abandoned. Not devastated. God who knows me, cares for me, lifts me, holds me. Taking full responsibility for my life, which I have yielded to Him.

JANUARY 20

HE IS *the* GOD *of* DETAILS

Yea, though I walk through the valley of the shadow of death, I will fear no evil: for Thou art with me; Thy rod and Thy staff they comfort me. Thou preparest…

PSALM 23:4–5 KJV

Thou: God of details. God who provides. God of Abraham. My God. Jehovah-Jireh. The One who sees, knows, cares.

preparest: Every place prepared before I arrive; every provision met before I am even aware of what I need. Not haphazard. Not unplanned. God ordered. God ordained. God maintained. God sustained. All things set in dazzling array, in its proper place, for its proper purpose, in its proper time. The plans of His heart being revealed to me.

January 21

He Gives You Daily Bread

Yea, though I walk through the valley of the shadow of death, I will fear no evil: for Thou art with me; Thy rod and Thy staff they comfort me. Thou preparest a table…

PSALM 23:4–5 KJV

A **table:** God's table. A daily table. A forever table. A table set by Him. His gathering place. His dining place. His banqueting place. Beautifully arranged. Abundantly filled. A place of feasting, of communion, of pleasures forevermore. A place where I can linger. A place to speak of His victories, to celebrate His joys, to learn of His ways, to share in the things that delight His heart and mine. A place where I can taste and see that the Lord is good.

January 22

Enjoy His Presence Moment *by* Moment

Yea, though I walk through the valley of the shadow of death, I will fear no evil: for Thou art with me; Thy rod and Thy staff they comfort me. Thou preparest a table before me...

PSALM 23:4-5 KJV

Before me: My special place. Reserved, complete with my own nametag. The perfect spot. Seated right next to Him. Receiving my portion directly from His hand. Leaning my head against His breast. Knowing I belong. Knowing I am right where I need to be, right where I want to be, right where I was made to be—breaking bread at the family table.

January 23

He Is *the* Victor *and* Your Victory

Yea, though I walk through the valley of the shadow of death, I will fear no evil: for Thou art with me; Thy rod and Thy staff they comfort me. Thou preparest a table before me in the presence of mine enemies...

PSALM 23:4-5 KJV

In the presence of mine enemies: Not in la-la land. Not in a make-believe world where difficulties, temptations, and the forces of evil do not exist. Being in His light while surrounded by darkness; feasting upon His truth though lies and deception lurk in the shadows; receiving His affirming love while voices of accusation and condemnation cry out to get my attention. Knowing He is for me even though the enemy comes against me. Certain that no foe can keep me out, shut me out, or cut me off from what He has prepared at His table. Certain He is enough.

January 24

His Face Shines *upon* You

Thou preparest a table before me in the presence of mine enemies: Thou anointest my head with oil...
PSALM 23:5 KJV

Thou: Abba, Father. The One who calls me His own. God of every invitation to be where He is. The One who says, "Come follow Me," "Come be with Me," "Come know Me." The Host of all hosts, greeting me with welcome arms.

anointest my head with oil: Anointed by my King and High Priest. Anointed with the oil of gladness. Equipped. Enabled. Empowered. Holy oil—making my face to shine; causing my heart to sing; softening my hands to touch others. Refreshing my life, restoring my soul, renewing my spirit—protecting me from being sun-parched, shielding me from all that would crack, dry, deplete, blister. Fresh oil. Ever flowing. Ever being poured out upon me.

January 25

He Is *the* Source *of* Overflowing Goodness

Thou preparest a table before me in the presence of mine enemies: Thou anointest my head with oil; my cup runneth over.

PSALM 23:5 KJV

My cup: Earthen cup. Heart-shaped. Cup of need. Cup of longing. Cup of thirsting after Him. Lifted up for filling. Lifted up to receive. Cup of trust, cup of faith. Cup of asking, cup of drinking. Cup of blessings, cup of everlasting joy.

runneth over: God of abundance! Not drip-drops. Not trickles. Not small portions. Not rations. Not squeezing out a little moisture from His promises. God of the rivers of living water. God of the waterfalls of grace. God of the overflow. Allowing me to drink of everything pure, everything good, everything right, everything true, everything satisfying, everything that flows from His heart to mine.

January 26

God Will Not Fail You

Thou preparest a table before me in the presence of mine enemies: Thou anointest my head with oil; my cup runneth over. Surely...

PSALM 23:5–6 KJV

Surely: No "I wonder?" No "I wish!" No "I hope so." Without a doubt. Without a question. Without a concern or worry. Knowing whose I am and who He is. God of His word, God of His promise. God of His covenant. God of His oath. God who cannot and will not fail, falter, or forget.

January 27

Your Life Couldn't Be *in* Better Hands

Thou preparest a table before me in the presence of mine enemies: Thou anointest my head with oil; my cup runneth over. Surely goodness...
PSALM 23:5-6 KJV

Goodness: Not meanness. Not cruelty. Not unkindness. His goodness. The goodness of God—the goodness in His nature, the goodness in His character, the goodness in His being. Everything about Him good—every thought, every action, every attitude, every decision, every work, every word. Good in His will. Good in His gifts. Good to me. Good every moment. Good all the time. Extending goodness—not as little as He can give, but as much as He can give. Being the best, giving the best, wanting the best. Delighting to shower me with His graciousness—time after time, over and over, now and forevermore.

JANUARY 28

YOU ARE COVERED *in* KINDNESS

Thou preparest a table before me in the presence of mine enemies: thou anointest my head with oil; my cup runneth over. Surely goodness and mercy...

PSALM 23:5-6 KJV

And mercy: Sweet mercy! Welcomed friend! Wonderful companion! New every morning. Fresh from His heart. Lifting condemnation. Releasing my past. Breaking my chains. Freeing my spirit. Renewing my hope. Securing my future. Mercy upon mercy. Mine in abundance. Kindly extended. Beautifully given. Graciously bestowed.

January 29

He Is Your Security

Thou preparest a table before me in the presence of mine enemies: Thou anointest my head with oil; my cup runneth over. Surely goodness and mercy shall follow me…

PSALM 23:5–6 KJV

Shall follow me: Not "there's a good possibility." Not "a 50/50 chance." Will follow! Never to retreat, abandon, or flee. Absolute certainty. Promised by the God who cannot lie. His benefits and blessings—mine to receive. Mine to enjoy. Mine to celebrate. Keeping me from being defeated. Guarding me from being pulled back into my past. Protecting me from being overtaken by things I cannot control. His divine escorts on my pilgrim journey.

January 30

Every Day *of* Your Life Is His Day

Thou preparest a table before me in the presence of mine enemies: Thou anointest my head with oil; my cup runneth over. Surely goodness and mercy shall follow me all the days of my life...

PSALM 23:5–6 KJV

All the days of my life: Not once in a while. Not hit-or-miss. Not off-and-on. Not just on good days. Not just on church days. All my days—cloudy days. Stormy days. Busy days. Quiet days. Days filled with joy. Days filled with sorrow. Days when I feel up. Days when I feel down. Every day. Every moment. Every step. Every breath. Every heartbeat.

January 31

The Best Is Coming *and* Will Always Be

Thou preparest a table before me in the presence of mine enemies: Thou anointest my head with oil; my cup runneth over. Surely goodness and mercy shall follow me all the days of my life: and I will dwell in the house of the Lord for ever.

PSALM 23:5–6 KJV

And I will dwell in the house of the Lord forever: The forever place—not temporary, not momentary, not transitory. The Father's house. My reserved place. My prepared place. Home! Never to be kicked out, evicted, or left homeless. The place my faith has thought upon. The place my hope is set upon. The place where I belong. The place I was made for. Jesus' place. The place where I am welcomed. The place where I am received. Mine by inheritance. Mine by grace. Mine forever and ever. In the company of the redeemed. In the presence of the Lord. Seeing Him face to face. Knowing even as I am known. Completely fulfilling all my heart has ever longed for...more than I could ever ask or think.

FEBRUARY 1

JESUS REACHES OUT *to* TOUCH YOU

He [Jesus] put forth His hand, and touched him.
LUKE 5:13 KJV

He reaches out to the sick and brings healing.

He reaches out to the hungry and provides bread.

He reaches out to the guilty and extends mercy.

He reaches out to the repentant and brings forgiveness.

He reaches out to the lepers and makes them clean.

He reaches out to the fearful and gives them peace.

He reaches out to the brokenhearted and binds their wounds.

FEBRUARY 2

JESUS REACHES OUT *to* BLESS YOU

He [Jesus] put forth His hand, and touched him.

LUKE 5:13 KJV

He reaches out to the sorrowful and gives them comfort.

He reaches out to the discouraged and gives them hope.

He reaches out to the weak and makes them strong.

He reaches out to the humble and gives them grace.

He reaches out to the childlike and draws them close to His heart.

He reaches out to those in despair and brings them the hope of His salvation.

He reaches out to the needy and gives them His blessing.

February 3

God's Grace Is Beyond Words

God is able to make all grace abound toward you; that ye, always having all sufficiency in all things, may abound to every good work.
II CORINTHIANS 9:8 KJV

Grace is truly a word that goes beyond description. Grace is not God's "a little bit more." Grace is God's "so much more." How much more? More than you could ever ask for, more than you could ever think about, more than you could ever grasp, hope, or dream.

FEBRUARY 4

PRECIOUS PROMISES *of* BOUNDLESS GRACE

Consider these Scriptures that speak about the "much more" gift of God's indescribable, overflowing grace toward you today.

Consider the ravens, for they neither sow nor reap, which have neither storehouse nor barn; and God feeds them. Of how much more value are you than the birds?
(LUKE 12:24 NKJV).

But if this is how God clothes the grass which is in the field today and tomorrow is thrown into the furnace, how much more will He clothe you? You of little faith!
(LUKE 12:28 AMP).

For if when we were enemies we were reconciled to God through the death of His Son, much more, having been reconciled, we shall be saved by His life
(ROMANS 5:10 NKJV).

February 5

Grace That Responds to Need

His father said to the servants, "Quick! Bring the finest robe in the house and put it on him. Get a ring for his finger and sandals for his feet. And kill the calf we have been fattening. We must celebrate with a feast."

LUKE 15:22–23 NLT

Consider the following about the father's response to his son returning:

Not: Waiting on the front porch. But: Running to meet him.

Not: A handshake. But: An embrace.

Not: Bring him something nice to wear. But: Bring him the best robe.

Not: Here's a list of things to do in order to get back in my graces. But: Here is the ring of my authority, power, and favor.

Not: Let's go get a hamburger. But: Let's prepare the fatted calf. It's time for a feast.

Not: Your return makes me smile. But: Let us celebrate for you were lost but now you are found.

February 6

Graciously Gracious

All things are for your sakes, that the abundant grace might through the thanksgiving of many redound to the glory of God.

II CORINTHIANS 4:15 KJV

God is not grudgingly gracious, He is graciously gracious. His grace brings Him great joy. You are saved by grace, transformed by grace, redeemed by grace, strengthened by grace, kept by grace, sanctified by grace, blessed by grace, have become an heir by grace, and have moment-by-moment access to God's throne of grace. Grace is God's free, flowing, flourishing favor. Grace brings to you the eternal riches in Christ and all that will remain forever.

February 7

Truth Keeps You *in* Balance

Whatever you do in word or deed, do all in the name of the Lord Jesus, giving thanks to God the Father through Him.
COLOSSIANS 3:17 NKJV

Truth does not hop around on one foot. It walks forward on two strong, well-balanced legs. Jesus *taught* the truth and *lived* the truth.

Sometimes we can put an emphasis on "doing" and make that the most important thing, and sometimes we can put the emphasis on "teaching" and make that the most important thing. One of these truths must never be emphasized at the expense of the other. As believers in Christ, we are called to live the Gospel and preach the Gospel; demonstrate the Kingdom and proclaim the Kingdom; do good works and teach good doctrine; live a life of love and speak the truth in love.

FEBRUARY 8

ACTIONS THAT SPEAK GOOD THINGS

You are the salt of the earth.... you are the light of [Christ to] the world.
MATTHEW 5:13–14 AMP

In Matthew 5:13–14 Jesus tells His disciples that they are *both* the salt of the earth and the light of the world. They were not told to choose between the two. The difference between salt and light is significant. Jesus used salt and light as metaphors to help the disciples understand the importance of both their *actions* and their *words.*

When Jesus said to His disciples they were "the light of the world," He was speaking about the power and impact of their *actions* upon the lives of others. When Jesus called the disciples "the salt of the earth," He was speaking about the power and impact of their *words* upon the lives of others. May our actions and our words both be expressions of God's heart.

February 9

God Uses You *to* Bless Others

Let your speech at all times be gracious and pleasant, seasoned with salt, so that you will know how to answer each one [who questions you].

COLOSSIANS 4:6 AMP

Salt is a delightful additive to our taste buds. Used in proper amounts, it enhances the foods we eat and brings out their unique flavors.

Like salt, there are those who bring a special seasoning of the Spirit to our lives. They add the seasoning of hope, faith, and encouragement into conversations and relationships. Their presence enhances our lives whenever we are with them. They say the words that are exactly what our hearts need to hear. Words of life, words of truth, and words of grace are words of salt that come from the heart of God.

February 10

God Uses You *to* Help Others

Let him seek peace and pursue it.

I PETER 3:11 NKJV

As a preservative, salt keeps things safe from injury, destruction, or decay. Before the days of refrigeration, salt was used by commercial fishing boats to keep their catch fresh until they could return to port and bring the fish to market.

Our homes, our workplaces, our marriages, our friendships, and our churches all need the preserving power of the Holy Spirit working through us. As the salt of the earth, we can be an influence for good and help keep marriages from being destroyed, businesses from becoming corrupted, and ministries from being overtaken by deadness and decay. As the salt of the earth, we can help to keep things sound and secure; healthy and protected; prosperous and blessed.

FEBRUARY 11

GOD USES YOU *to* BUILD UP OTHERS

The tongue of the wise brings healing.
PROVERBS 12:18 NIV

Do you have a wound? Add salt water to it and it will help to cleanse the injury and keep the body safe from infection. Whether you soak in salt water or gargle it, its healing power will go to work instantly.

Salt is vital to the health of our bodies. Without the proper amount of salt we would suffer greatly. God has made our bodies dependent upon salt to maintain optimum health, vitality, and even life itself. Salt helps regulate the heart and keeps our blood flowing.

Sometimes we don't fully see or understand the benefits we bring to others as the salt of the earth. The Body of Christ needs saltiness to remain free of deception and lies, discouragement and listlessness, carelessness and sin.

FEBRUARY 12

HIS WORDS *for* TODAY'S NEED

Thy words were found, and I did eat them; and Thy word was unto me the joy and rejoicing of mine heart: for I am called by Thy name, O LORD God of hosts.

JEREMIAH 15:16 KJV

Do you need comfort? Let His words console you.

Do you need guidance? Let His words give you wisdom.

Do you need encouragement? Let His words bring you hope.

Do you need gladness? Let His words delight you.

Do you need stillness? Let His words speak peace to you.

Do you need confidence? Let His words build you up.

Do you need daily bread? Let His words feed your hungry heart.

February 13

Redemption

Let the words of my mouth and the meditation of my heart be acceptable and pleasing in Your sight, O Lord, my [firm, immovable] rock and my Redeemer.

PSALM 19:14 AMP

Father, thank You for Your redemption. Jesus, thank You for being my Redeemer. Holy Spirit, thank You for Your redeeming work, for Your holiness, and for conforming me to the image of Jesus Christ. I cannot thank You enough, Father, Son, and Holy Spirit for turning the ashes in my life into something beautiful. I stand amazed at the wonders You continue to do in me by Your grace, and for the transforming miracles that I experience because of Your daily mercies. I trust in You to use every trial in my life for the good. May the beauty of Jesus continue to be seen in me.

February 14

The Word *of* God

Your words were found, and I ate them,
and Your word was to me the joy and
rejoicing of my heart; for I am called by
Your name, O Lord God of hosts.

JEREMIAH 15:16 NKJV

When you need illumination, it's a lamp to your feet.

When you need guidance, it's a light to your path.

When you encounter spiritual warfare, it's the sword of the Spirit.

When you are hungry, it's your daily bread.

When you need refreshment, it's the rejoicing of your heart.

February 15

God Will Never Betray His Own

As for God, His way is perfect; the word of the Lord is proven; He is a shield to all who trust in Him.

PSALM 18:30 NKJV

God will never betray our trust in what He has said, and as we wait upon Him to fulfill His promises, we do not need to fear disappointment. Since what God has for us will exceed our expectations, it means we can never expect too much.

The reality of His promises will far exceed what your faith is trusting Him to do. As you wait for the fulfillment of His promises, you don't have to wait in gloom or misery. Even if you don't understand the things that are happening around you, you can celebrate with joy and abundant praise for what He will one day reveal and fully accomplish.

FEBRUARY 16

LIVE *in the* ATMOSPHERE *of* PEACE

I will hear what God the LORD will speak,
for He will speak peace to His people.
PSALM 85:8 NKJV

Joy is like a flame of the Holy Spirit within us. Fretting is like a giant fire extinguisher that quenches the flame.

The peace of God is the atmosphere that He wants you to live in. Guard against letting the news headlines of the day carry you outside the atmosphere of God's peace.

FEBRUARY 17

THREE CHILD-LIKE HEART ATTITUDES *of* KINGDOM GREATNESS

So anyone who becomes as humble as this little child is the greatest in the Kingdom of Heaven.

MATTHEW 18:4 NLT

Humility: Humility is a disposition that says, "There is no greatness in me." Little children are not concerned about their status, title, or how much they know. As kingdom people our prayer should be, "Lord, help me to be less so You can be more."

Dependency: Little children are dependent upon another to provide for them, guide them, protect them, and care for them. As kingdom people we are as dependent upon the Lord as a branch is upon the vine.

Trust: Little children live in simplicity. Life isn't complicated. They don't live under a cloud of doubt. As kingdom people we live by faith, and our trust is fully in the Lord.

February 18

How Great He Is

For the Lord is a great God And a great King above all gods.

PSALM 95:3 AMP

The song of the kingdom is not "How Great We Are," it is "How Great He Is." Kingdom greatness is found in God Himself—His is the kingdom, and the power, and the glory forever! Our greatness is found in having the childlike characteristics of humility, dependency, and trust in the Lord that allow us to discover His greatness.

Little children live in a place of discovery. They are little explorers who find wonder and amazement around every corner. Our greatest adventure of faith in God's kingdom is discovering His thoughts and His ways.

February 19

His Desire Is *to* Bless You

Blessed be the God and Father of our Lord Jesus Christ, who has blessed us with every spiritual blessing in the heavenly places in Christ.

EPHESIANS 1:3 NKJV

You will never lack anything that His grace cannot give you, and He will give to you over and over again. Because His supply is abundant you will never be without. Because His heart is full you will never be empty. Because His resources are endless there will never be a time when He cannot meet your needs. Your life couldn't be in better hands. As you come to Him in prayer remember how much He desires to bless you.

February 20

He Is Your Constant Companion

I will be to Israel like a refreshing dew from heaven. Israel will blossom like the lily; it will send roots deep into the soil like the cedars in Lebanon.

HOSEA 14:5 NLT

The Lord daily brings you to pastures green with life and nourishment, cool with delight and refreshing, pleasant with freedom and beauty. It is a place of rest to quiet your heart…a place of hope to renew your spirit…a place of joy to delight your soul. You are so blessed to be able to share the Lord's pleasant company today.

FEBRUARY 21

LIVE *in* HIS REST

In God I have put my trust, I shall not be afraid.
PSALM 56:11 NASB

In your quiet times or busy times God has a quiet place for you to rest.

As you gaze upon the waters of the Holy Spirit, you will see the reflection of His face. His waters are present to wash you, delight you, and refresh you. They will bring you rest from all your fears, worries, cares, and anxieties. In His quiet place there is no weight upon you, no confusion around you, and no clouds over you. It is the place where you can peacefully open your heart to Him.

February 22

It Is Well *with* Your Soul

Oh, sing to the Lord a new song!
PSALM 98:1 NKJV

It is delightful to come before the Lord in quietness, in adoration, and in prayer. As you kneel at His feet and gaze upon His face, renewal gently comes. In your weariness you will be refreshed, in your weakness your strength will be renewed, in your heaviness your heart will sing a new song. His wings will be your covering, His faithfulness will be your shield, His lovingkindness will be your sweet reward. Beautiful are His ways with you.

FEBRUARY 23

GOD HEARS *and* ANSWERS PRAYER

My voice You shall hear in the morning,
O LORD; in the morning I will direct
it to You, and I will look up.
PSALM 5:3 NKJV

As you walk the paths of prayer you will be guided into everything that is true and right...into all that is best for you and others...into all that will take you to the highest expressions of His love. He will lead you by His way, by His words, and by His will. He will guide you down the paths that lead you straight to His heart. Each prayer He answers will be for your good and for His glory.

February 24

Nothing Is Better *than* His Presence

Because Your lovingkindness is better than life, my lips shall praise You.

PSALM 63:3 NKJV

The greatest thing your heart can experience with God is His presence. He is greater than any of His gifts. What He is to you is greater than anything He can do for you. His lovingkindness is better than life…in His presence is fullness of joy…at His right hand are pleasures forevermore. When God gives Himself to you there is nothing higher or greater He can give.

February 25

God Will Comfort You

O may Your lovingkindness and graciousness comfort me, According to Your word (promise) to Your servant.

PSALM 119:76 AMP

Comfort in prayer comes by knowing that the One you look to is always looking out for you. He is not only with you, but He is actively doing everything that is necessary to keep you safe within His care. You can be assured that above you are His tender mercies... around you is His unfailing love...underneath you are His everlasting arms.

FEBRUARY 26

YOU HAVE SO MUCH GOING FOR YOU

You prepare a table before me in the presence of my enemies.

PSALM 23:5 AMP

Even though you may have a lot of things that come against you, you have so much more going for you. While your enemies try to rob you of your joy, God spreads a lavish table before you filled with spiritual blessings of goodness, kindness, and love. As you come to Him in prayer you find a table your soul can delight in...your faith can feast upon...and your heart can rejoice in. His table is never empty.

FEBRUARY 27

YOU ARE BLESSED *with the* HOLY SPIRIT

You anoint my head with oil.
PSALM 23:5 NKJV

When you come to God in times of personal dryness or when you are in need of help or healing, you will find His loving hand pouring out the anointing oil of His Spirit upon you—comforting, refreshing, and filling you. His oil heals and soothes, calms and relieves, and causes His face to shine upon you.

FEBRUARY 28

HE RESPONDS *to* YOUR PRAYERS

Because He bends down to listen, I will pray as long as I have breath!

PSALM 116:2 NLT

How glorious and wonderful are the things you discover about God's heart when you are in prayer—kindness, beauty, goodness, mercy, grace, favor, blessings, faithfulness, and lovingkindness. In His great generosity He has given to you freely, bountifully, cheerfully. He has given you the finest, the highest, the deepest, and the fullest measure of His love. All that He has given He will continue to give to you all the days of your life.

MARCH 1

HARDSHIPS WORKING *for the* GOOD

I am the true vine, and My Father is the vinedresser.

JOHN 15:1 NKJV

God is working all things together for a greater good:

Wheat is crushed before it is turned to bread.

Incense is cast upon the fire before the fragrance within is set free.

Soil feels the blade of the plow before the seed is planted.

Pressure is applied before the diamond can be formed.

Irritants are added before pearls are created.

Gold is refined before it becomes pure.

Wine is poured from vessel to vessel before its taste is sweet.

Vines are pruned before they produce much fruit.

March 2

The Lord Is Near

He Himself has said, "I will never leave you nor forsake you."
HEBREWS 13:5 NKJV

What could be sweeter or dearer than to know that no one is nearer to your heart, your soul, or your deepest desires than the Lord. His caring eyes are upon you, His protecting hands are over you, His assuring voice speaks peace to you, His loving heart responds to you. You can come to Him in quietness and confidence, in faith, in hope, in trust, in thanks, in worship, in praise, and in prayer.

MARCH 3

TAKE HIS EASY YOKE

Come unto Me, all ye that labour and are heavy laden, and I will give you rest. Take My yoke upon you, and learn of Me; for I am meek and lowly in heart: and ye shall find rest unto your souls. For My yoke is easy, and My burden is light.

MATTHEW 11:28–30 KJV

Beautiful in all Your splendor,
I yield to You in full surrender.
I turn from all that's not your best,
And take my place within Your rest.
Strife and worry, all must cease,
When I'm abiding in Your peace.
I take Your yoke, there is no toil,
Lord, pour on me Your holy oil.

MARCH 4

LORD, SPEAK *through* ME

A word fitly spoken is like apples
of gold in pictures of silver.
PROVERBS 25:11 KJV

Lord, speak through me the soothing words that will heal a hurting heart; the wise words that will guide a seeking heart; the assuring words that will comfort a grieving heart; the accepting words that will embrace a lonely heart; the affirming words that will strengthen a fearful heart; the life-giving words that will fill an empty heart.

March 5

The Glory *of the* Cross

But far be it from me to boast except in the cross of our Lord Jesus Christ, by which the world has been crucified to me, and I to the world.
GALATIANS 6:14 ESV

The cross tells us:
We are sinners and need a Savior.
We are lost and need to be found.
We are guilty and need mercy.

The cross points us to Jesus:
His shed blood cleanses us.
His grace justifies us.
His finished work makes us whole.

The cross assures us:
Jesus is the only way.
God's love held nothing back.
We have been bought with a price.

March 6

Jesus Died *for* You

God demonstrates His own love toward us, in that while we were still sinners, Christ died for us.

ROMANS 5:8 NKJV

The message of the cross is a message of God's amazing love and grace. The Bible tells us that Jesus died *for you.*

Jesus dying for you is a glorious truth. He died for your sins. He took your sins upon Himself. He was your sacrificial lamb. His blood made atonement for you.

He was your substitute, dying in your place—taking your judgment, your death, your hell. He died as your Redeemer, shedding His blood to buy you back to God as His possession, and to bring you the heart-freeing joy of knowing Him.

March 7

Jesus Rose *for* You

Who is he who condemns? It is Christ
who died, and furthermore is also risen,
who is even at the right hand of God,
who also makes intercession for us.

ROMANS 8:34 NKJV

Jesus died and rose for us! Does this not say it all?

If we only knew this one truth, it would be sufficient.

If we only had this loaf of spiritual bread to eat, it would satisfy our hunger.

If we only had this living water to drink, it would quench our thirst.

Jesus died and rose for you!

This is the taproot from which the tree of life grows.

This is the headwater from which the healing river flows.

This is the pen from which the great doctrines of faith are written—justification, sanctification, redemption, salvation—Jesus died and rose for you.

March 8

Yes, God Loves You!

He who did not spare [even] His own Son, but gave Him up for us all, how will He not also, along with Him, graciously give us all things?

ROMANS 8:32 AMP

Does God love you?

Yes, Jesus died and rose for you.

Does God care about you?

Yes, Jesus died and rose for you.

Does God provide for you?

Yes, Jesus died and rose for you.

Does God forgive you, save you, and receive you?

Yes, Jesus died and rose for you.

March 9

You Are My Peace (Part 1)

Peace I leave with you, My peace I give to you; not as the world gives do I give to you. Let not your heart be troubled, neither let it be afraid.

JOHN 14:27 NKJV

Lord, You are Jehovah-Shalom. Thank You for Your peace. Shalom peace. Perfect peace. What a precious gift You have given me through Your peace. Where would I be without the blessing of Your peace in my life?

Help me to know the reassuring, confirming voice of Your peace in my daily decisions and choices. I trust You to guide me and keep me with the peace that passes understanding.

March 10

You Are My Peace (Part 2)

Now may the Lord of peace Himself give you peace always in every way.

II THESSALONIANS 3:16 NKJV

Father, You are the author of peace...may Your peace be written upon my heart.

Jesus, You are the Prince of Peace...may Your peace rule over my heart.

Holy Spirit, You are the river of peace...may Your peace flow abundantly in my heart.

MARCH 11

THE IMPORTANCE *of* FAITH

Faith is the confidence that what we hope for will actually happen; it gives us assurance about things we cannot see....And it is impossible to please God without faith. Anyone who wants to come to Him must believe that God exists and that He rewards those who sincerely seek Him.

HEBREWS 11:1, 6 NLT

Faith is the hand that reaches up, takes ahold of God's promise, and gathers in the spiritual treasures that are found in Christ.

What things are possible for you today through faith? All things are possible, because your faith is in the God who knows no impossibilities.

MARCH 12

ALL THINGS ARE POSSIBLE

Jesus said to him, "If you can believe, all things are possible to him who believes."

MARK 9:23 NKJV

When your resources don't match your need, faith says, "God is my provider." When you are fearful to take the next step, faith says, "God will not fail me." When you're not sure what to do next, faith says, "God will guide me."

When you are in a situation that seems impossible, faith says, "Nothing is too hard for the Lord."

When the things that you are experiencing don't make sense, faith says, "God knows what He is doing."

March 13

God Has Promised (Part 1)

Because of His glory and excellence, He has given us great and precious promises. These are the promises that enable you to share His divine nature and escape the world's corruption caused by human desires.

II PETER 1:4 NLT

Know the promises: God has spoken promises to us. Those promises are recorded in Scripture so we can know what is in His heart toward us. His promises will keep us from praying amiss. His promises are not fleeting words of emotion, they are words of truth. Without the truth of His promises we could be overcome with superstition, timidity, and anxiety. It is because of His promises that we can live a life of freedom, confidence, and contentment.

March 14

God Has Promised (Part 2)

All of God's promises have been fulfilled in Christ with a resounding "Yes!" And through Christ, our "Amen" (which means "Yes") ascends to God for His glory.

II CORINTHIANS 1:20 NLT

Pray the promises: In addition to the importance of knowing God's promises is the importance of praying His promises. When we buy a car we are also given a key. Without the key the car just sits. Even when we insert the key, we still must turn the key to get things moving. Prayer is like turning the key, it puts the promises into motion (Luke 11:9–13).

March 15

God Has Promised (Part 3)

"God is not a man, that He should lie, Nor a son of man, that He should repent. Has He said, and will He not do it? Or has He spoken and will He not make it good and fulfill it?

NUMBERS 23:19 AMP

Trust the heart of the Promise Giver: We will not have the confidence we need to pray unless we trust in the character of the One who has spoken the promises. Often people who make promises to us also tell us to trust them. They may be sincere in their request, but even the best intentions are flawed by human weakness, forgetfulness, and limited resources.

There are no flaws in God's character and no empty words in His promises. We can be thankful that as we ask for our daily bread, we do not call upon a God with human weaknesses or limitations, but upon the One who loves us with a perfect love and has promised to supply all our needs from His glorious riches that have been given to us in Jesus Christ.

March 16

Surrendering to God's Rest

I appeal to you therefore, brothers, by the mercies of God, to present your bodies as a living sacrifice, holy and acceptable to God, which is your spiritual worship.

ROMANS 12:1 ESV

In order for us to fully surrender we must understand who we are surrendering to. We are not surrendering our lives to a mean tyrant, to an uncaring person, or to a capricious creator. We need to see our surrender as a surrender to perfect love.

The meaning of full surrender is simply stated in the following quote by François Fénelon:

It is simply resting in the love God, as a little baby rests in its mother's arms. Surrender consists, not in doing great, heroic deeds about which self can brag, but simply in accepting whatever God sends, and not seeking to change it (unless it is His will for it to be changed). Full surrender is full peace.

MARCH 17

RUN *to* JESUS

The name of the LORD is a strong tower;
the righteous run to it and are safe.
PROVERBS 18:10 NKJV

Is there a trial you are facing, a difficulty you are walking through, a sorrow you are carrying?

You are not alone in these trying times. There is One alone who is a very present help in time of need. In Jesus you have a Warrior who has won the battle, a Champion who has defeated the foe, a Conqueror who will lead you in triumph.

He is your Light in the darkest night, your Companion in the deepest valley, your Guide through the densest forest, your Rock on the shakiest ground, your Shelter from the strongest storm, your Oasis in the driest desert, your Captain on the roughest seas.

Run to Jesus! Run to His love. Run to His strength. Run in confidence. Run with all your heart.

March 18

Love Found *a* Way

And be found in Him, not having my own righteousness, which is from the law, but that which is through faith in Christ, the righteousness which is from God by faith.

PHILIPPIANS 3:9 NKJV

I came with my struggles and found Your peace,
I came with my bondage and found Your release.
I came with my burdens and found Your care,
I came with my loneliness and found You there.

I came with my weakness and found You strong,
I came with my sadness and found Your song.
I came with my questions and found You true,
I came with my old ways and found things new.

March 19

If

What then shall we say to these things? If God is for us, who can be against us?

ROMANS 8:31 NKJV

If He weren't exalted, I would be down!
If He weren't my joy, I'd be wearing a frown.
If He weren't guiding, I'd stay in my seat.
If He weren't victorious, I'd live in defeat.

If He weren't the Master, where would I go?
If He weren't the Healer, who'd mend my soul?
If He weren't the Teacher, how could I learn?
If He weren't the Answer, where would I turn?

If He weren't the High Priest, I wouldn't have a prayer.
If He weren't my peace, I'd be loaded with care.
If He weren't the Shepherd, I simply would roam.
If He weren't in heaven, I wouldn't have a home.

March 20

May You Find Jesus *to* Be...

For to me, to live is Christ [He is my source of joy, my reason to live] and to die is gain [for I will be with Him in eternity].

PHILIPPIANS 1:21 AMP

The music that causes your heart to sing;

The joy that causes your heart to rejoice;

The glory that causes your heart to worship;

The wonder that causes your heart to believe;

The security that causes your heart to trust;

The peace that causes your heart to rest;

The promise that causes your heart to hope;

The beauty that causes your heart to delight;

The majesty that causes your heart to surrender;

The love that causes your heart to give.

March 21

When You Need Him Most

Can anything ever separate us from Christ's love? Does it mean He no longer loves us if we have trouble or calamity, or are persecuted, or hungry, or destitute, or in danger, or threatened with death?... No power in the sky above or in the earth below—indeed, nothing in all creation will ever be able to separate us from the love of God that is revealed in Christ Jesus our Lord.

ROMANS 8:35, 39 NLT

His strongest grace is for your weakest moment;

His sweetest fellowship is for your loneliest journey;

His richest supply is for your neediest hour;

His closest embrace is for your deepest sorrow;

His brightest light is for your darkest day.

March 22

It's All about Jesus

And he is the head of the body, the church. He is the beginning, the firstborn from the dead, that in everything he might be preeminent.

COLOSSIANS 1:18 ESV

It's not about living for Jesus; it's about letting Jesus live in us. John 15:5

It's not about improving ourselves; it's about Jesus transforming us. Luke 9:23

It's not about our self-image; it's about Jesus' glory. I Corinthians 10:31

It's not about our abilities; it's about Jesus' power. Acts 1:8

It's not about our inconveniences; it's about Jesus' cross. Hebrews 4:9

It's not about our resources; it's about Jesus' riches. II Corinthians 9:6

It's not about our recognition; it's about Jesus' approval. John 8:29

March 23

Praise

Therefore by Him let us continually offer the sacrifice of praise to God, that is, the fruit of our lips, giving thanks to His name.

HEBREWS 13:15 NKJV

Praise to You, Lord God Almighty! You are good. Kind. Gracious. You are love, and full of compassion. I am blessed to spend each day in Your presence.

You are greater than all there is, greater than all that there has been, and greater than all that will ever be. I sing unto You, for You are my song; I rejoice in You, for You are my celebration; I delight in You, for You are my greatest treasure.

Moment by moment, and day by day, You are my Savior and my God!

March 24

Keep On Trusting

Trust in Him at all times.

PSALM 62:8 NLT

Putting your trust in the Lord is a full-time, lifelong, joy-filled privilege. Put your trust in the Lord when you have much and when you have little; when things are going smooth and when things are going rough; when you are settled and when you are in the midst of change; when you have understanding and when you aren't sure what to do.

Trust in the Lord is not seasonal or selective, optional or debatable, relative or arbitrary. Trust in the Lord should be steadfast, constant, consistent, unwavering. You can completely trust in the One who is completely trustworthy.

March 25

There Is...

The Spirit of the Lord will rest on Him—
the Spirit of wisdom and understanding,
the Spirit of counsel and might, the Spirit
of knowledge and the fear of the Lord.
ISAIAH 11:2 NLT

For the journey there is guidance:

I will instruct you and teach you in the way
you should go; I will guide you with My eye.
PSALM 32:8 NKJV

For the walk there is endurance:

May the Lord lead your hearts into a full
understanding and expression of the love of God
and the patient endurance that comes from Christ.
II THESSALONIANS 3:5 NLT

For the task there is strength:

Be strong in the Lord and in
the power of His might.
EPHESIANS 6:10 NKJV

March 26

Receive His Benediction

Now to Him who is able to do exceedingly abundantly above all that we ask or think, according to the power that works in us, to Him be glory in the church by Christ Jesus to all generations, forever and ever. Amen.

EPHESIANS 3:20–21 NKJV

May you receive from the Lord Jesus Christ, who is mighty and abundant in you, every blessing, every kindness, and every provision of life to be abundantly joyful, exceedingly peaceful, extremely hopeful, and overwhelmingly grateful for His abounding grace and favor toward you.

March 27

In Jesus...

In Him dwells all the fullness of the Godhead bodily; and you are complete in Him.
COLOSSIANS 2:9–10 NKJV

In Jesus...

The poor find riches,
The weak find strength,
The broken find wholeness,
The heavy-laden find rest,
The sorrowful find comfort,
The embattled find victory,
The captives find liberty,
The weary find refreshment,
The tempted find escape,
The bound find freedom,
The empty find fullness,
The hungry find bread,
The downcast find joy.

March 28

The Lord's Provision Is Complete

In all these things we are more than conquerors and gain an overwhelming victory through Him who loved us.

ROMANS 8:37 AMP

For every hectic work day there is a quiet rest...

For every painful experience there is a healing touch...

For every negative feeling there is an abiding joy...

For every disappointment there is a certain hope...

For every turbulent storm there is a sure foundation...

For every doubting thought there is a calm assurance...

For every hurtful action there is a forgiving love.

March 29

Great Is *the* Lord

Give thanks to the Lord and proclaim His greatness. Let the whole world know what He has done. Sing to Him; yes, sing His praises. Tell everyone about His wonderful deeds. Exult in His holy name; rejoice, you who worship the Lord. Search for the Lord and for His strength; continually seek Him. Remember the wonders He has performed, His miracles, and the rulings He has given, you children of His servant Abraham, you descendants of Jacob, His chosen ones.

PSALM 105:1–6 NLT

Today, may you love Him as your Father,

Thank Him as your Creator,

Look to Him as your Guide,

Depend upon Him as your Protector,

Trust in Him as your Provider,

Seek Him as your Strength,

Yield to Him as your Lord,

Worship Him as your God,

Serve Him as your King.

March 30

God Is...All You Need

He Himself gives life and breath to everything, and He satisfies every need.
ACTS 17:25 NLT

You can't save yourself, God is your Savior. Luke 1:47

You can't justify yourself, God is your Justifier. Romans 3:24

You can't redeem yourself, God is your Redeemer. Psalm 78:35

You can't cleanse yourself, God is your Cleanser. Psalm 51:2

You can't deliver yourself, God is your Deliverer. Psalm 70:5

You can't perfect yourself, God is your Perfecter. Psalm 138:8

You can't keep yourself, God is your Keeper. Psalm 121:5

You can't comfort yourself, God is your Comforter. II Corinthians 1:3

March 31

All He Is, He Is *for* You

In Him all the treasures of [divine] wisdom (comprehensive insight into the ways and purposes of God) and [all the riches of spiritual] knowledge and enlightenment are stored up and lie hidden.

COLOSSIANS 2:3 AMP

Provider: You are satisfied.
Teacher: You are instructed.
Shelter: You are covered.
Rock: You are secure.
Victor: You are triumphant.
Shepherd: You are cared for.
Captain: You are protected.
Encourager: You are built up.
Salvation: You are delivered.
Healer: You are whole.
Rest: You are comforted.
Guide: You are directed.
Confidence: You are assured.
Father: You are accepted.
Deliverer: You are free.

April 1

Ten Things You Will Never Receive *from* God (Part 1)

God has not given us a spirit of fear and timidity, but of power, love, and self-discipline.

II TIMOTHY 1:7 NLT

Second best. Psalm 34:10

Temptation to do evil. James 1:13

A half-hearted love. Jeremiah 31:3

Indifference. Luke 13:34

Forgetfulness. Isaiah 49:15

Insufficient grace. II Corinthians 9:8

Unnecessary discipline. Hebrews 12:5–6

A depleted supply of blessings. Ephesians 1:3

Watered down truth. Psalm 19:7–8

Compromise. Hebrews 6:17–18

April 2

Ten Things You Will Never Receive *from* God (Part 2)

The Lord keeps you from all harm and watches over your life.

PSALM 121:7 NLT

Unavailability. Psalm 86:7

Incomplete salvation. Hebrews 7:25

Lukewarmness. Isaiah 9:7

Unkindness. Psalm 63:3

Confusion. I Corinthians 14:33

Desertion. Hebrews 13:5

Unwise counsel. I Corinthians 1:19–31

Empty promises. II Corinthians 1:20

Bad timing. Psalm 18:30

An uncaring heart. I Peter 5:7

April 3

As God's Child, Who Is against You?

If God is for us, who can ever be against us?
ROMANS 8:31 NLT

God is not against you.

Jesus is not against you.

The Holy Spirit is not against you.

The angels are not against you.

They are greater than any foe that is against you.

It is God who has the final authority

and the final say over everything that concerns you.

April 4

Prayer *of* Service

We ourselves are your servants for Jesus' sake.

II CORINTHIANS 4:5 NLT

God, here are my hands; work through them as I give myself to Your assigned tasks. Here is my voice, speak Your words through me as I follow Your promptings. Here are my feet; guide them in the paths of righteousness as I obey Your leading. Here is my heart; fill it with the love that bears all things, believes all things, hopes all things, endures all things…the love that never fails—for Your glory. Amen.

April 5

The Humble Place

I restore the crushed spirit of the humble and revive the courage of those with repentant hearts.

ISAIAH 57:15 NLT

God's grace works within our lives to strip us and reduce us, to mold us and shape us, to conform us into His image, and to transform us into His likeness. God reveals to us our true needs and causes us to see how truly dependent we are upon Him. God does this, not to leave us empty, but to fill us with His true riches found in Jesus Christ; not to leave us downcast, but to be our glory and the lifter of our heads; not to make our lives miserable, but to bring to us the fullness of His joy; not to make our lives meaningless, but to work within us His eternal purpose.

April 6

He Reduces *to* Increase

He prunes the branches that do bear fruit
so they will produce even more.
JOHN 15:2 NLT

Don't be discouraged today if you sense God's hand doing its sanctifying work in your life. If He is trimming your wick, it is only to make your light shine brighter; if He is allowing you to be pressed within His caring hands, it is only to release the flow of the sweet wine of His Spirit.

Humble yourself under His mighty hand, and as you do, allow this prayer to be upon your lips:

Father, work in me what I cannot work; do in me what I cannot do; be in me what I cannot be; live through me what I cannot live—for I know it is through You, and You alone, that my life will be to the praise of Your glory.

APRIL 7

NOT ABILITY *but* AVAILABILITY

Also I heard the voice of the Lord, saying: "Whom shall I send, and who will go for Us?" Then I said, "Here am I! Send me."

ISAIAH 6:8 NKJV

When we say "not me" we place the focus upon ourselves, our limitations, and weaknesses. However, faith says, "God can." God can use me, gift me, empower me, and be to me all I need.

Gideon told God, "I can't," but God told Gideon, "You can because I have sent you and I will be with you." When you have Him you have all you need!

April 8

The Lord Will Use You

He [God] said, "I have appeared to you for this purpose, to make you a minister and a witness both of the things which you have seen and of the things which I will yet reveal to you."... I was not disobedient to the heavenly vision.

ACTS 26:16, 19 NKJV

When we say to God, "Yes, use me," that does not mean that our obedience of faith is complete. We, by faith, have the opportunity to add this commitment to our prayer, "Yes, Lord, use me now, in this moment, if it is Your time." God wants to use us in His appointed time, not ours. We cannot live a life of faith and put things off for another day if God says, "Do it now," and we do not want to rush ahead if God says, "Wait."

April 9

The Lord Knows Where *to* Place You

Jesus…said to him, "Go home to your friends, and tell them what great things the Lord has done for you."

MARK 5:19 NKJV

Sometimes we think we can serve God better and more effectively if we are somewhere else and with other people. We can think, *I will serve You, Lord, when You send me to the mission field; I will let my life be a witness for You when I am with strangers, but not when I am with my family and friends here at home.* God wants you to trust Him to work through you in the place He has you. He wants to work through you to touch the people who are around you now.

April 10

God's Way Is *the* Best Way

Nevertheless not My will, but Yours, be done.

LUKE 22:42 NKJV

We cannot lean upon our own understanding; we must lean upon the arm of the Lord. When David was about to face Goliath, Saul told David to do it his way, using his armor; David refused and did it God's way (dependent upon the Lord) and faced the enemy with a sling and a stone. God's ways are not our ways. Our faith must respond to what God wants us to do and how He wants us to do it. One plus God is always a majority!

April 11

Important Questions Concerning God's Will

Who are those who fear the Lord? He will show them the path they should choose.

PSALM 25:12 NLT

If God isn't leading you to a certain place, why go there?

If God hasn't asked you to do a certain task, why perform it?

If God hasn't directed you to speak a certain word, why declare it?

If God wouldn't be pleased with a certain choice, why choose it?

April 12

Heartfelt Responses Concerning God's Will

The name of our Lord Jesus will be glorified in you [by what you do], and you in Him, according to the [precious] grace of our God and the Lord Jesus Christ.

II THESSALONIANS 1:12 AMP

If God isn't leading you to a certain place, why go there? Lord, I am following You. I will not run around in circles trying to find my own way. I place my feet in Your footsteps.

If God hasn't asked you to do a certain task, why perform it? Lord, I will only carry what You ask me to lift. I lay down my agenda and my ideas.

If God hasn't directed you to speak a certain word, why declare it? Lord, put Your words in my mouth. I want to speak words that are fitting for the moment—the right word, the true word, the word from Your heart to others.

APRIL 13

MORE IMPORTANT QUESTIONS ABOUT GOD'S WILL

Who are those who fear the LORD? He will show them the path they should choose.

PSALM 25:12 NLT

If what you're seeking is moving you away from God's heart, why pursue it?

If the outcome is not God's best, why settle for it?

If God has told you to wait, why push forward?

If God has told you to go, why hold back?

April 14

More Heartfelt Responses Concerning God's Will

Let love be your greatest aim.

I CORINTHIANS 14:1 TLB

If what you're seeking is moving you away from God's heart, why pursue it? Lord, I turn my back to all that would turn me away from You. I come to You, I run to You, I press in to know You more and to lay hold of the purpose for which You laid hold of me.

If the outcome is not God's best, why settle for it? Lord, I refuse to be content with a life that is run-of-the-mill. I choose the best that love has to give—I choose You.

If God has told you to wait, why push forward? Lord, I lay down my pushiness, my desire to control and manipulate people and circumstances in order to have things turn out the way I want them to.

APRIL 15

GOD IS CHANGELESS

I am the Lord, I do not change.

MALACHI 3:6 AMP

God never changes. He is perfect—without flaw, error, inconsistency, mistake, or poor judgment. God is not moody. He is always righteous. His goodness, His purity, His holy nature, His justice, and His character are eternal.

Knowing that God is changeless means that you can fully trust Him and wholly obey Him.

God did not begin to love man when Jesus came. Jesus came to roll back the curtain and show man the heart that was eternal, the love that was always there.

—G. Campbell Morgan

April 16

The Yoke *of* Jesus

I delight to do Your will, O my God.
PSALM 40:8 NKJV

If you are heavy laden, come and receive Jesus' easy yoke; if you are stressed, come and receive Jesus' light burden; if you are weary, come and receive Jesus' rest. When you are yoked to Jesus you are *not* yoked to heaviness, drudgery, or despair.

APRIL 17

JESUS in the CENTER

For to me, to live is Christ [He is my source of joy, my reason to live] and to die is gain [for I will be with Him in eternity].

PHILIPPIANS 1:21 AMP

Jesus is the Way. He is not only the Way to God, but He is the Way into all that God has for us. He is the Way into our devotions, to our Bible reading, to our prayer life, to our ministry, and to all that we do for Him. In reality, we do not do our work for Him, but He does His work through us. With Jesus in the center of our being, we are no longer victims of our expectations, circumstances, and the things we can't control. We discover that it's okay if people don't meet our expectations, because Jesus is our expectation. Schedules may be good, but they don't produce life within us because Jesus is our life. Don Lessin

From the booklet "Abba Cry" by Don Lessin

April 18

God's Love *for* You

The Lord has appeared of old to me, saying:
"Yes, I have loved you with an everlasting love;
therefore with lovingkindness I have drawn you."
JEREMIAH 31:3 NKJV

Child of God, how does He love you?
He loves you—
With an everlasting love;
With a perfect love;
With a pure love;
With a sacrificial love;
With an unfailing love;
With a steadfast love;
With a kind love;
With a forgiving love;
With an accepting love;
With an all-embracing love;
With an enduring love;
With a truthful love;
With a holy love;
With a gracious love;
With a patient love.

April 19

God's Heart Draws You *to* His Heart

Then Christ will make His home in your hearts as you trust in Him. Your roots will grow down into God's love and keep you strong. And may you have the power to understand, as all God's people should, how wide, how long, how high, and how deep His love is. May you experience the love of Christ, though it is too great to understand fully. Then you will be made complete with all the fullness of life and power that comes from God.

EPHESIANS 3:17–19 NLT

God loves you:

With a love that reaches to the heights,

With a love that goes to the depths,

With a love that calls you,

Draws you, keeps you,

And holds you close to His heart.

APRIL 20

TODAY, CHOOSE *the* BEST

Choose today whom you will serve.
JOSHUA 24:15 NLT

The best over the acceptable, the right over the popular, the true over the questionable, the light over the shadowed, the extraordinary over the mediocre, the eternal over the momentary, the pure over the tainted, Jesus over all!

April 21

Found *in* Him

I also count all things loss for the excellence of the knowledge of Christ Jesus my Lord, for whom I have suffered the loss of all things, and count them as rubbish, that I may gain Christ and be found in Him.

PHILIPPIANS 3:8–9 NKJV

Jesus is above all things, and He transcends all things—being found in Him means that you have found completeness! Nothing is missing, nothing is lacking, nothing falls short, nothing fails, and nothing disappoints that is found in Him, for all that we find in Him is perfectly good, perfectly right, and perfectly wonderful.

April 22

Where Would We Be *without* Jesus?

Yes, I am the vine; you are the branches. Those who remain in Me, and I in them, will produce much fruit. For apart from Me you can do nothing.

JOHN 15:5 NLT

Without Jesus' words we would be witnesses with nothing to say; without Jesus' authority we would be ambassadors with nothing to do; without Jesus' love we would be servants with nothing to give.

I am not strong, but I receive Him who is made unto me wisdom, righteousness, sanctification, and redemption. In absolute dependence on the Savior, we exemplify that growing sense of need that is one of the sure signs of the humble and contrite heart that God will not despise.

—*F. B. Meyer*

April 23

Words *to* Share His Heart

My tongue is the pen of a ready writer.

PSALM 45:1 NKJV

Hear what the Spirit is saying.

Write holy words.

Overflow with goodly themes.

Declare freeing truth.

Speak in gracious tones.

Dip your pen in the ink of light.

Write as expectantly as the dawning of a new day, as boldly as the brightness at high noon, and as tenderly as the hues painted across the sky at sunset.

Write with the light that causes kingdom seeds to grow.

Write words that dance like starlight, beam like moonlight, and glow like candlelight, even on the darkest night.

Be a ready writer.

April 24

Jesus, *the* Champion

Wonderful Counselor, Mighty God,
Everlasting Father, Prince of Peace. His
government and its peace will never end.
ISAIAH 9:6–7 NLT

Jesus is the Champion of all champions…no one comes close! All His titles are eternal; He has always held them, and no one in heaven or on earth has ever taken them away…no one ever will. His throne, His greatness, His glory, His dominion, His authority, and His kingdom are settled forever. Leave all with Him, place all before Him, trust all to Him.

April 25

His Wonderful Name

The name which is above every name.

PHILIPPIANS 2:9 AMP

Wonderful Counselor: Place yourself at His feet, hear His words, follow His wisdom, go with His plan, yield to His strategy. Do not set any limits upon what He can *say to you.*

Mighty God: What a King! Warrior. Victor. Lord. Without flaw or weakness. Clothed with glory. Crowned with majesty. Do not set any limits upon what He can *do for you.*

Everlasting Father: He is the best. Kindest. He is full of compassion. Grace. Lovingkindness. Draw close to Him. Walk with Him. He is always the same. Do not set any limits upon what He can *be to you.*

Prince of Peace: He is Peace. Perfect peace. He can use you as His peacemaker in a restless and troubled world. Do not set any limits upon what He can *do through you.*

April 26

Great Grace

And great grace was upon them all.
ACTS 4:33 NKJV

What is the reality that God wants you to see today? He has handed you a glass that is filled to the brim with grace. He says that He has given you "all" grace and "all" sufficiency in "all" things. To put it simply, your victory today has nothing to do with the power of positive thinking, but it has everything to do with the power of His grace. God is not saying, "Have a positive attitude about My provision for you even though My provision for you is lacking and not complete." God is saying, "Put your *faith* in My sufficiency. I have given you all you need. My grace abounds toward you. I have given you a 'grace-glass' that is overflowing!"

April 27

A Prayer of Blessing for Children (Part 1)

May the Lord bless you and protect you.
May the Lord smile on you
and be gracious to you.
May the Lord show you His favor
and give you His peace.
NUMBERS 6:22–26 NLT

Here is a prayer of blessing to pray over your children based upon Numbers 6:22–26:

Father, my heart is full of praise to You for blessing me with the gift of my beautiful children. I want to say, "Thank You so much!" Your blessings leave me in awe. You have enriched my life in more ways than I could ever imagine.

Your blessing, Father, means everything. My prayer and deep desire is that my children will be blessed of the Lord. May Your blessing be upon them. As Aaron spoke Your blessing over the people of Israel, so I speak Your blessing over my children today.

April 28

A Prayer *of* Blessing *for* Children (Part 2)

So I say to you, ask, and it will be given to you; seek, and you will find; knock, and it will be opened to you. For everyone who asks receives, and he who seeks finds, and to him who knocks it will be opened.

LUKE 11:9–10 NKJV

Father, bless my children with Your favor and kindness; keep them by Your power and strength, and deliver them from all evil; may Your face shine upon them with the light of Your radiant love; may they know the abundant riches of Your amazing grace; lift up upon them the smile of Your countenance; shield their hearts and minds with Your abiding peace, the perfect peace that passes all understanding.

APRIL 29

RECEIVING *and* WAITING

Then you will not become spiritually dull and indifferent. Instead, you will follow the example of those who are going to inherit God's promises because of their faith and endurance.

HEBREWS 6:12 NLT

In your walk with God two things will always be true: You will be receiving from Him and you will be waiting upon Him. Your faith must trust Him for both. You need to receive from Him what is yours for today and wait upon Him for what will be yours tomorrow.

What are things that are yours today? His peace, His grace, His mercies, His forgiveness, His cleansing, His strength, His presence, His life, His blessing, His love.

There are also things that require your faith to wait. They include prayers you are waiting to see answered, promises you are waiting to be fulfilled, and God's timing in relation to your personal guidance.

April 30

The Rest *of* Faith

Wait patiently for the Lord. Be brave and courageous. Yes, wait patiently for the Lord.

PSALM 27:14 NLT

What should your faith do in response to what is yours today? Receive! What should your faith do in response to what will be yours another day? Rest!

As you wait upon the Lord, wait with a thankful heart, not a complaining one; with a peaceful heart, not a striving one; with a confident heart, not an uncertain one; with a patient heart, not a hasty one.

You do not need to try to manipulate your future. God is able to fulfill all that He has promised. As you wait, continue to pray, continue to trust, continue to believe, continue to hold hope in your heart, continue to obey, and continue to rejoice evermore. You have a God who cannot and will not fail!

May 1

Blessed *by the* Blessed One

According to the glorious gospel of the blessed God which was committed to my trust.

I TIMOTHY 1:11 NKJV

The God and Father of our Lord Jesus Christ, who is blessed forever.

II CORINTHIANS 11:31 NKJV

His blessings bring sunshine and rain, seedtime and harvest, flowers and songbirds, and a thousand other things we experience throughout life. However, there is something greater than having God's blessings, and that is having the blessing of *God Himself*, the One who is blessed forever.

MAY 2

YOUR GREATEST TREASURE

We have this treasure in earthen vessels, that the excellence of the power may be of God and not of us.

II CORINTHIANS 4:7 NKJV

You may not have a lot of money, but you have incredible wealth. You may not have an abundance of things, but you possess more than you could ever ask or think. God has placed within you the greatest treasure anyone can ever possess—it is the life of Jesus Christ. He has freely lavished upon you a treasure house of good things that you can freely give away to others.

May 3

A Benediction

This is the way to have eternal life—to know You, the only true God, and Jesus Christ, the One You sent to earth.

JOHN 17:3 NLT

May you continue to hear His voice more clearly, know His heart more deeply, rest in His care more fully, trust His faithfulness more completely, walk His pathway more confidently, know His presence more intimately, and be blessed by His favor more abundantly.

May 4

Clean Hands *and* *a* Pure Heart

Who may climb the mountain of the Lord? Who may stand in His holy place? Only those whose hands and hearts are pure, who do not worship idols and never tell lies. They will receive the Lord's blessing and have a right relationship with God their Savior.

PSALM 24:3–5 NLT

Psalm 24:3–5 speaks about clean hands and a pure heart. Our hands will be clean as we allow God to work through us, and our hearts will be pure as we allow God to work within us:

Clean hands impact our actions; a pure heart impacts our attitudes.

Clean hands will be seen by others; a pure heart will be seen by God.

Clean hands will do right things; a pure heart will do them for the right reasons.

May 5

Truths *about* Prayer

Now this is the confidence that we have in Him, that if we ask anything according to His will, He hears us.
I JOHN 5:14 NKJV

God's understanding of your need is much greater than your ability to express it. *Don't be like them, for your Father knows exactly what you need even before you ask Him! Matthew 6:8 NLT.*

Cares that come are not to be carried but released into God's hands. *Casting all your care upon Him, for He cares for you. I Peter 5:7 NKJV.*

The power in prayer is not found in the eloquence of the one who prays but in the power of God who answers. *And do not lead us into temptation, but deliver us from the evil one. For Yours is the kingdom and the power and the glory forever. Amen. Matthew 6:13 NKJV.*

May 6

Living *for* Kingdom Purposes

So use your whole body as an instrument to do what is right for the glory of God.
ROMANS 6:13 NLT

The life of every believer in Christ is set apart from a worldly purpose to a kingdom purpose; from impure living to holy living; from unrighteous actions to righteous actions; from selfish choices to loving choices; from wanting our own way to following His way; from pleasing ourselves to doing what is pleasing in His sight.

May 7

You Are Set Apart

You were cleansed; you were made holy; you were made right with God by calling on the name of the Lord Jesus Christ and by the Spirit of our God.

I CORINTHIANS 6:11 NLT

You have not been set apart to be neglected, to be empty and alone, to be useless and fruitless, to be mistreated and abused. You have been set apart by the Lord, *for the Lord*. He wants you all to Himself, without rival in your heart. He wants you to enjoy Him wholly, serve Him completely, and know Him fully.

You have been set apart for fellowship and for companionship with Him. You are His sanctified vessel—with a high and holy calling, with an eternal hope and purpose, with a divine commission to make Him known, and with an inheritance that is beyond the reach of decay, reserved in heaven for you.

May 8

Blessed Assurance

I can do everything through Christ,
who gives me strength.

PHILIPPIANS 4:13 NLT

May Jesus assure you that as you follow Him you will never meet a fear He cannot conquer; you will never face an enemy He cannot defeat; you will never enter a battle He cannot win; you will never have a need He cannot meet; you will never face a temptation He cannot overcome; you will never have a burden He cannot lift; you will never face a problem He cannot solve; you will never have a bondage He cannot break; you will never have a moment when He does not care; you will never have a time when He is not there.

May 9

The Future

Now all glory to God, who is able, through His mighty power at work within us, to accomplish infinitely more than we might ask or think. Glory to Him in the church and in Christ Jesus through all generations forever and ever! Amen.

EPHESIANS 3:20–21 NLT

Jesus is your future.

He has called you to follow Him with a heart of faith and a life of obedience. In good times, in troubled times, or in uncertain times, all your times are in His hands. Your future is filled with God's promises. It is a future as hopeful as the faithfulness of God; as secure as the character of God; as abounding as the grace of God; as abundant as the love of God.

May 10

Being Still *to* Know His Will

The likeness of the firmament above the heads of the living creatures was like the color of an awesome crystal, stretched out over their heads.... And when they stood still, they let down their wings. A voice came from above the firmament that was over their heads; whenever they stood, they let down their wings.

EZEKIEL 1:22, 24–25 NKJV

"Flapping wings" is a picture of activity. It can be good activity; it can even be activity in the Lord's work. However, we all need those times when we quiet ourselves before the Lord. "Letting down our wings" means quieting ourselves and being still before the Lord to hear His voice. It is a good thing to be still and know that He is God.

May 11

There Is Hope

I have formed you, you are My servant; O Israel, you will not be forgotten by Me! I have blotted out, like a thick cloud, your transgressions, and like a cloud, your sins. Return to Me, for I have redeemed you.

ISAIAH 44:21–22 NKJV

You can turn back to God, because He has not turned His back on you.

You can hold on to God, because He has not released His hold on you.

You can love God, because He has never stopped loving you.

May 12

Leaving All *for* His All

Indeed I also count all things loss for the excellence of the knowledge of Christ Jesus my Lord, for whom I have suffered the loss of all things, and count them as rubbish, that I may gain Christ.

PHILIPPIANS 3:8 NKJV

From the book *God Calling* by A. J. Russell we find this statement: "Leave all to Me." Although this statement is not a direct quote from Scripture, it is in agreement with Scripture. Let these words sink deep into our hearts.

God, who is our all in all, wants us to leave our all with Him—all our cares, all our burdens, all our fears, all our worries. He also wants us to leave our hopes, our expectations, our needs, and our very lives with Him.

May 13

What About?

Casting all your care upon Him,
for He cares for you.
I PETER 5:7 NKJV

God wants you to cast all your care upon Him, but what about…

Your plans?

Leave them with Him.

Your possessions?

Leave them with Him.

Your relationships?

Leave them with Him.

Your desires?

Leave them with Him.

May 14

Leave It All *with the* Lord

I know whom I have believed and am persuaded that He is able to keep what I have committed to Him until that Day.

II TIMOTHY 1:12 NKJV

What about…

Your career?

Leave it with Him.

Your security?

Leave it with Him.

Your ministry?

Leave it with Him.

Your future?

Leave it with Him.

Give everything *to* the Lord, and leave everything *with* the Lord.

May 15

Since

He hath on His vesture and on His thigh a name written, King of kings, and Lord of lords.
REVELATION 19:16 KJV

Since Jesus is the way, shouldn't He be followed?

Since Jesus is the truth, shouldn't He be believed?

Since Jesus is the life, shouldn't He be enjoyed?

Since Jesus is wise, shouldn't He be consulted?

Since Jesus is God, shouldn't He be worshiped?

Since Jesus is King, shouldn't He be obeyed?

Since Jesus is Lord, shouldn't He have the final say?

May 16

How *to* Respond *to* God's Will

I take joy in doing Your will, my God, for Your instructions are written on my heart.
PSALM 40:8 NLT

Wholeheartedly. *Whatever you do, do your work heartily, as for the Lord rather than for men. Colossians 3:23 NASB.*

Joyfully. *Serve the LORD with gladness. Psalm 100:2 KJV.*

Faithfully. *Well done, thou good and faithful servant. Matthew 25:21 KJV.*

When God reveals His will to you, embrace it as a wonderful privilege, acknowledge it as something you *get to do*! The Psalmist said this about God's will: "I take joy in doing Your will."

May 17

Reasons *to* Come *to* Jesus

Jesus replied, I assure you, most solemnly I tell you, before Abraham was born, I AM.

JOHN 8:58 AMP

Jesus is the Savior, come to Him and be forgiven and saved. Luke 2:11

Jesus is the Door, come to Him and enter His provision. John 10:9

Jesus is the Bread of Life, come to Him and feast at His table. John 6:51

Jesus is the Light of the World, come to Him and see clearly. John 8:12

Jesus is the Good Shepherd, come to Him and be led in right paths. John 10:14

Jesus is the Vine, come to Him and abide in fruitfulness. John 15:5

Jesus gives living water, come to Him and drink to the full. John 4:10

Jesus is the Resurrection, come to Him and have hope. John 11:25

Jesus gives peace, come to Him and be not troubled. John 14:27

May 18

Be

Oh, the joys of those who do not follow the advice of the wicked, or stand around with sinners, or join in with mockers. But they delight in the law of the Lord, meditating on it day and night. They are like trees planted along the riverbank, bearing fruit each season. Their leaves never wither, and they prosper in all they do.

PSALM 1:1–3 NLT

Be renewed (Ephesians 4:23), be transformed (Romans 12:2), be conformed (Romans 8:29), be steadfast (I Corinthians 15:58), be faithful (I Corinthians 4:2), be strong (Ephesians 6:10), be filled (Ephesians 5:18), be diligent (II Peter 3:14), be holy (I Peter 1:15), be content (I Timothy 6:8), be kind (Ephesians 4:32), be thankful (Colossians 3:15), be gentle (II Timothy 2:24), be patient (James 5:7), be watchful (Revelation 3:2), be ready (Matthew 24:44), be to the praise of His glory (Ephesians 1:12).

MAY 19

FAITHFUL PROMISES

As surely as God is trustworthy and faithful and means what He says... For as many as are the promises of God, they all find their Yes [answer] in Him [Christ].

II CORINTHIANS 1:18, 20 AMP

Here are four things that you can be certain of about God's promises:

1. God never forgets a promise He has made.
2. What God promises He is fully able to do.
3. He never promises something He never intended to do.
4. He never gets side-tracked from fulfilling His promises.

May 20

Who Jesus Really Is

Who do the people say that I am?

LUKE 9:18 NASB

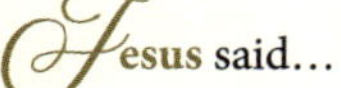

Jesus said…

1. I am the Bread of Life. John 6:35–51
2. I am the Light of the World. John 8:12, 9:5
3. I am the Door of the Sheep. John 10:7–9
4. I am the Good Shepherd. John 10:11–14
5. I am the Resurrection and the Life. John 11:25
6. I am the Way, the Truth, and the Life. John 14:6
7. I am the True Vine. John 15:1–6

Ask Him to be to you all that He is, according to your need today.

May 21

God Has Chosen You

You didn't choose me. I chose you. I appointed you to go and produce lasting fruit.

JOHN 15:16 NLT

God was the one who formed you, gave you the breath of life, and brought you into the world. He did this so that His arms could embrace you and His love could keep you. He wanted you to know that your relationship with Him would always be of more value than the things He would have you do for Him. He wanted you to be certain that He loved you completely before you ever did anything in His service, so that your service would never become a way of trying to earn His love or favor.

May 22

You Are *the* Lord's

Fear not, for I have redeemed you; I have called you by your name; You are Mine.

ISAIAH 43:1 NKJV

As you came to know His heart and hear His voice, you heard Him speak a call to your life. This call would mean that He would never ask you to do anything for Him that He expected you to do without Him. He alone would be your sufficiency. His only desire is that you daily open your heart to His resources—never saying "I can't" without also saying "He can!"

You are now in the place He has called you. He has made no mistakes in leading you. Even in the hard places He is working out what is best—not only for you and for others but also for His kingdom.

May 23

He Knows Your Heart

The Lord sees not as man sees; for man
looks on the outward appearance,
but the Lord looks on the heart.
I SAMUEL 16:7 AMP

He is not looking at your statistics or programs to measure you; He is looking at your heart. Be assured that it is His presence that will keep you and make you strong.

You are in God's place at God's perfect time. Your days are in His hands, and He is your future. He has gifted you and placed His hand upon you to bless you and make you a blessing. The burden of your ministry is not yours to carry—as you rest, He will work; as you abide, He will bring fruit; as you sow, He will give the increase. He is your shield and your exceeding great reward.

May 24

The Lord Is Your Friend

No longer do I call you servants, for a servant does not know what his master is doing; but I have called you friends, for all things that I heard from My Father I have made known to you. You did not choose Me, but I chose you and appointed you that you should go and bear fruit, and that your fruit should remain, that whatever you ask the Father in My name He may give you.

JOHN 15:15–16 NKJV

He is your provider. He will take care of you. He will nurture and sustain you. His Spirit is the wind to cool you, the water to refresh you, the power to enable you, the oil to anoint you, and the river that flows through you to touch the lives of others. Continue to be God's vessel, in God's place, doing God's will, in God's way, and always remember—God has chosen you!

May 25

Still

Before the mountains were brought forth, or ever You had formed the earth and the world, even from everlasting to everlasting, You are God.

PSALM 90:2 NKJV

In a dark world, His light still shines;
In a sinful world, His mercy still forgives;
In an unclean world, His blood still washes clean;
In a selfish world, His cross still redeems;
In a hurting world, His hands still heal;
In a grieving world, His embrace still comforts.

In a confusing world, His truth still frees;
In a lost world, His footsteps still lead the way;
In a weary world, His yoke still gives rest;
In an empty world, His presence still brings fullness of joy!

May 26

Reasons *to* Come *to* Jesus

Jesus told him, "I am the way, the truth, and the life. No one can come to the Father except through me."

John 14:6 NLT

Jesus is the Counselor, come to Him and be guided in His wisdom. Isaiah 9:6

Jesus is the Rabbi, come to Him and be instructed in righteousness. John 3:2

Jesus is the Life, come to Him and abundantly live. John 14:6

Jesus is the Great Physician, come to Him and be made whole. Matthew 14:36

Jesus is the Lord, come to Him and serve Him with gladness of heart. John 13:14

Jesus is the Son of God, come to Him and worship and adore Him. Matthew 14:33

May 27

Knowing *the* Names *of the* Lord

Blessed be the name of the Lord from this time forth and forevermore!

PSALM 113:2 NKJV

His name: King

Our response: Worship

His name: Lord

Our response: Surrender

His name: Almighty

Our response: Trust

His name: Provider

Our response: Believe

His name: Shepherd

Our response: Rest

May 28

His Names Are Glorious

Nor do those who pass by say,
"The blessing of the Lord be upon you;
We bless you in the name of the Lord.

PSALM 129:8 AMP

His name: Counselor
Our response: Listen

His name: Comforter
Our response: Lean

His name: Keeper
Our response: Abide

His name: Eternal One
Our response: Hope

His name: Victor
Our response: Overcome

May 29

His Names Are Dear *to the* Heart

They looked to Him and were radiant; Their faces will never blush in shame or confusion.

PSALM 34:5 AMP

His name: Life

Our response: Delight

His name: Guide

Our response: Follow

His name: Healer

Our response: Receive

His name: Creator

Our response: Celebrate

His name: Abba

Our response: Honor

May 30

How He Wants You *to* Be

These things I have spoken unto you, that in Me ye might have peace. In the world ye shall have tribulation: but be of good cheer; I have overcome the world.

JOHN 16:33 KJV

Followers of Jesus Christ have always faced trials, testing, hardships, and persecutions. When Jesus spoke about the times in which we are living, He had these things to say about how our hearts should be:

Be standing firm.

Be watchful.

Be peaceful.

Be prayerful.

Be sober.

Be ready.

May 31

Do Not Be Troubled

Peace I leave with you, My peace I give to you; not as the world gives do I give to you. Let not your heart be troubled, neither let it be afraid.

JOHN 14:27 NKJV

When Jesus spoke about the times in which we are living, He told us what not to be:

Do not be spiritually asleep.

Do not be fearful.

Do not be troubled.

Do not let your heart be weighed down with cares.

The Lord's kingdom is coming and He will reign forever and ever.

June 1

Living *by* Faith

The just shall live by his faith.
HABAKKUK 2:4 KJV

God wants us to live as those who trust Him fully. We can be those who live amidst fear yet have peace; who live amidst sorrow yet have comfort; who live amidst trouble yet have courage; who live amidst uncertainty yet have hope.

We are those who live in this world but are not of it; who face difficulties and overcome them; who face hardships and walk through them.

We are those who have not put our faith in our faith but in the faithfulness of God. God is our shield, refuge, high tower, and defender. Our trust is in God's character, our confidence is in God's ways, and our hope is in God's promises.

June 2

Shalom Peace

Gideon built an altar to the Lord there and named it Yahweh-Shalom (which means "the Lord is peace").

JUDGES 6:24 NLT

May you know the *shalom* peace of God—encouraging you to move forward, empowering you to boldly take each step, greeting you as you turn a new corner, calming your heartbeat as you walk through dark valleys, softening each footstep as you climb rugged mountains, and increasing your courage as you follow your Shepherd wherever He leads.

June 3

Answered Prayer

I cried out to the Lord, and He answered me from His holy mountain.

PSALM 3:4 NLT

You can pray because your Father in heaven has ears to hear, eyes to see, a mind to know, a will to do, and a heart that understands your every need. You can pray with confidence, having complete assurance in the One who says that all things are possible. For the power of prayer is not found in the words of your prayer but in the power of God. Remember, "*The Lord is my rock, my fortress, and my Savior; my God is my rock, in whom I find protection. He is my shield, the power that saves me, and my place of safety (Psalm 18:2 NLT).*

June 4

The Center

Yes, everything else is worthless when compared with the infinite value of knowing Christ Jesus my Lord. For His sake I have discarded everything else, counting it all as garbage, so that I could gain Christ.

PHILIPPIANS 3:8 NLT

Jesus is the balancing point of life. He is the center of joy and giver of the peace that passes all understanding. He is at the heart of all contentment, and He is at the core of all completeness. He is the focal point of your faith and the epicenter from whom all blessings flow.

In all things and for all things you have Jesus. He is all wisdom, all power, all life, all love. To know Him, to treasure Him, and to have Him is to gain all.

June 5

Mercy (Part 1)

You are a chosen generation, a royal priesthood, a holy nation, His own special people, that you may proclaim the praises of Him who called you out of darkness into His marvelous light; who once were not a people but are now the people of God, who had not obtained mercy but now have obtained mercy.

I PETER 2:9–10 NKJV

With a dead end before us, Christ showed us the way;

When we walked in the nighttime, Christ brought us the day.

When our faces were hidden, Christ carried our shame;

When we felt so unwanted, Christ called out our name.

June 6

Mercy (Part 2)

Hear me, O Lord, for Your lovingkindness is good; turn to me according to the multitude of Your tender mercies.

PSALM 69:16 NKJV

With a cup that was empty, Christ brought us His well;

When facing destruction, Christ saved us from hell.

With our fate like a leper, Christ reached out to heal;

When we lived like a phony, Christ gave what was real.

June 7

Mercy (Part 3)

I will sing of the mercies of the Lord forever; with my mouth will I make known Your faithfulness to all generations. For I have said, "Mercy shall be built up forever; Your faithfulness You shall establish in the very heavens."

PSALM 89:1–2 NKJV

With our fists in defiance; Christ stretched out His hand;

When our footsteps were sinking, Christ helped us to stand.

With no hope or a future, Christ came from above;

When our hearts were depleted, Christ poured in His love.

June 8

Past Day. This Day. That Day.

Sing to the Lord, bless His name; proclaim the good news of His salvation from day to day.
PSALM 96:2 NKJV

In *past* days without the Lord we were filled with darkness; *this* day we are flooded with light; in *that* day we will behold His glorious appearing.

In *past* days without the Lord we were filled with confusion; *this* day we have His peace; in *that* day we shall dwell with the Prince of Peace.

In *past* days without the Lord we were without hope; *this* day we look for the coming of the Lord; in *that* day we will be forever with the Lord.

In *past* days without the Lord we were paupers; in *this* day we are royal ambassadors; in *that* day we will reign with the King.

June 9

He's Always There

Cast your burden on the Lord,
and He shall sustain you.
Psalm 55:22 NKJV

We can be thankful Jesus is "always there"—there in our need, there in our weakness, there in our struggles, there in our tears, there in our burdens.

When Jesus came, He didn't come to seek and save those who "had it all together." He didn't look for those who would place few demands upon Him. He didn't tell seekers He was a busy man and they needed to work things out for themselves.

Thankfully, Jesus welcomes us. He invites us to come to Him. He has assured us that when we come to Him, He will sustain us.

June 10

Through Prayer

Ask, and it shall be given you; seek, and ye shall find; knock, and it shall be opened unto you: for every one that asketh receiveth; and he that seeketh findeth; and to him that knocketh it shall be opened.

MATTHEW 7:7–8 KJV

You may not be mighty, but you can pray and see situations change by the hand of Him who is almighty. You may not know how to comfort or encourage someone who is hurting, but you can pray and touch the heart of Him who is the Father of all comfort. You may not know how to protect yourself from evil, but you can pray and allow God to be your shield and defender. You may not have a lot of resources, but you can pray and receive what you need from the treasure house of Him whose resources are unlimited.

June 11

A Healing Stream *through* Prayer

Then you will call upon Me and go and pray to Me, and I will listen to you.
JEREMIAH 29:12 NKJV

Pray that broken hearts will turn to Him for healing, that grieving hearts will turn to Him for comfort, and that lost hearts will turn to Him for the gift of salvation that is in Jesus Christ alone. His grace is still being extended, His mercies are still new every morning, and His arms are still outstretched to embrace every hurting heart.

June 12

In God We Trust

It is good for me to draw near to God: I have put my trust in the Lord GOD.

PSALM 73:28 KJV

We can trust in God—

His kingdom is unshakable.

His throne is incorruptible.

His glory is indescribable.

His Word is infallible.

His greatness is unsearchable.

His power is invincible.

His favor is invaluable.

His grace is inexpressible.

His love is undeniable.

June 13

Fullness *of* Joy

You have made him most blessed forever; You have made him exceedingly glad with Your presence.
PSALM 21:6 NKJV

The Bible tells us that God has given us richly all things to enjoy (I Timothy 6:17), yet the joy He has for us goes even deeper. He not only wants us to enjoy the things He gives us, but He wants us to experience joy in its fullest measure (John 15:11). To have God's blessings brings enjoyment, but to have God Himself brings more than enjoyment, it brings fullness of joy. Fullness of joy means having His presence in the midst of all the blessings He gives.

June 14

See Jesus

And my God shall supply all your need according to His riches in glory by Christ Jesus.

PHILIPPIANS 4:19 NKJV

He is the complete provision for everything that pertains to life and godliness (II Peter 1:3).

He alone is where we find every spiritual blessing (Ephesians 1:3).

The most important thing we can do for our faith is "look to Jesus" (Hebrews 12:2). Our faith does not grow by looking at our resources, our abilities, our achievements, our contacts, or our status. Great faith looks to Jesus alone.

Jesus is the starting point, the ending point, and every point in between regarding our faith. Looking to Jesus means that our faith can unpack its bags because it has found its home. Jesus is not our Savior in various things but in all things; not our Shepherd on certain days but every day; not our Peace in certain circumstances but in every circumstance of life.

June 15

He Is *the* Greatest Blessing

After these things the word of the Lord came unto Abram in a vision, saying, Fear not, Abram: I am thy shield, and thy exceeding great reward.

GENESIS 15:1 KJV

The joys that come from the blessings God gives you can only go so far. They are *from Him*, but they are *not Him*. He freely gives you all things to enjoy, but even more, He wants you to enjoy Him! It is in Him alone that you will know the greatest of all gifts and the richest of all blessings.

June 16

Live (Part 1)

Anyone who belongs to Christ has become a new person. The old life is gone; a new life has begun!
II CORINTHIANS 5:17 NLT

Live *in* Him. *As you therefore have received Christ Jesus the Lord, so walk in Him. Colossians 2:6 NKJV*

Live *through* Him. *Yet in all these things we are more than conquerors through Him who loved us. Romans 8:37 NKJV*

Live *from* Him. *For from Him and through Him and to Him are all things. To Him be the glory forever. Amen. Romans 11:36 NASB*

Live *with* Him. *Now if we died with Christ, we believe that we shall also live with Him. Romans 6:8 NKJV*

JUNE 17

LIVE (PART 2)

Jesus said to him, "You shall love the LORD your God with all your heart, with all your soul, and with all your mind."
MATTHEW 22:37 NKJV

Live *empowered* by Him. *He who says he abides in Him ought himself also to walk just as He walked. I John 2:6 NKJV*

Live *by* Him. *"Not by might nor by power, but by My Spirit," says the LORD of hosts. Zechariah 4:6 NKJV*

Live *for* Him. *Yet for us there is one God, the Father, of whom are all things, and we for Him; and one Lord Jesus Christ, through whom are all things, and through whom we live. I Corinthians 8:6 NKJV*

JUNE 18

MERCY, PEACE, *and* LOVE

May God give you more and more
mercy, peace, and love.
JUDE 1:2 NLT

Because of God's mercies you can follow Him with all of your heart today, assured that there is nothing being held over your head to condemn you. You can take each step today with a quiet heart knowing that His peace keeps you steady and sure. You can move ahead today with great confidence of faith knowing His love keeps you close to His heart, mindful of His promises, and confident of His care. God's mercies declare that you are covered in His compassion; His peace proclaims that you are renewed in His rest; His love heralds that you are bathed in His blessings of joy.

June 19

Patiently Endure

So be truly glad. There is wonderful joy ahead, even though you have to endure many trials for a little while.

I PETER 1:6 NLT

Do not lose heart. God knows and understands the difficulty you face.

Even the darkest night can be followed by the brightest new day. Matthew 28:1–3

Even the roughest storm can be followed by a calm sea. Mark 4:37, 39

Even the greatest trial can be followed by a song of deliverance. Exodus 15:1–2

June 20

Untangled Knots

Every valley shall be raised, And every mountain and hill be made low; And let the rough ground become a plain, And the rugged places a broad valley.

ISAIAH 40:4 AMP

Behold, I am the Lord, the God of all flesh. Is there anything too hard for Me?

JEREMIAH 32:27 NKJV

How are we to respond to problems we cannot solve, to differences we cannot reconcile, to difficulties we cannot fix, to heartaches we cannot heal, to tensions we cannot ease? The answer is not to struggle, to strive, or to attempt to work things out in our own wisdom and strength. These are the times when we need to remain hopeful, to renew our trust in the Lord, and to place things in His skilled hands. Only He can heal what we cannot mend, reconcile what we cannot restore, and untangle what we cannot untie.

June 21

Jesus, *the* Only One

Jesus said to him, "I am the way, the truth, and the life. No one comes to the Father except through Me."
JOHN 14:6 NKJV

Jesus is...

The only Way to God (John 14:6).

The only Door to enter (John 10:7–9).

The only Salvation to receive (Acts 4:12).

The only Living Bread to feast upon (John 6:35).

The only Truth to know (John 14:6).

The only Light to walk in (John 8:12).

The only Vine to abide in (John 15:1).

The only Life to live (John 14:6).

The only Good Shepherd to follow (John 10:14).

The only Sure Foundation to build upon (I Corinthians 3:11).

The only Mediator to call upon (I Timothy 2:5).

The only Lord to serve (I Corinthians 8:6).

June 22

Let

But let all who take refuge
and put their trust in You rejoice,
Let them ever sing for joy;
Because You cover and shelter them,
Let those who love Your name
be joyful and exult in You.

PSALM 5:11 AMP

Are you tired or weary today? Let God renew you with His strength.

Are you discouraged or downhearted? Let God lift you with His hand.

Are you carrying a burden of sin? Let God restore you with His touch.

Are you in need of reassurance? Let God hold you with His embrace.

Are you in need of healing? Let God mend you with His Word.

June 23

Thankful *for* Grace

God is able to make all grace abound toward you; that ye, always having all sufficiency in all things, may abound to every good work.

II CORINTHIANS 9:8 KJV

Lord, thank You for Your grace. It is by grace that my heart was drawn to You—grace that was extended, not in limited measure, but in abundance; not sprinkled down but poured out; not just enough to get me by but more than enough to bring me through as more than a conqueror.

Your grace brings me riches in my poverty; sufficiency in my inadequacy; abundance in my lack. I thank You for being so gracious—for Your heart of grace that is reaching out, and for Your gift of grace. Thank You for Your only begotten Son, who has embraced me in His arms of mercy, and who brings to me the fullness of grace and truth.

June 24

From Faith *to* Faith

Therein is the righteousness of God revealed from faith to faith: as it is written, The just shall live by faith.
ROMANS 1:17 KJV

The Gospel—where faith is grounded and becomes steadfast. Colossians 1:23

The sacred Scriptures—where faith responds in trusting obedience. Romans 16:26

The promises and faithfulness of God—where faith receives what is hoped for. Hebrews 11:1

The trials of life—where faith is refined and strengthened. I Peter 1:7

The fiery darts of doubt and unbelief—where faith fights the good fight and overcomes the evil one. I Timothy 6:12

The throne of grace—where faith draws near in prayer with full confidence. Hebrews 10:22

The Lord Jesus Christ—where faith begins its journey and finishes its course. Hebrews 12:2

June 25

Prayer *for* Patience

Set your mind on things above,
not on things on the earth.
COLOSSIANS 3:2 NKJV

Jesus, thank You for sending the Holy Spirit to me. Thank You that the Holy Spirit is the source and the river of Your life being lived in me. Thank You that I can fully and confidently trust in the work of the Holy Spirit in my life, for the Holy Spirit's nature is exactly the same as Yours.

Holy Spirit, I yield to Your control. I receive the fruit of Your patience. I turn away from the attitude that insists things must work out according to my timetable and my expectations. Bring me into agreement with Your perfect timing in my life. Produce in me a quiet heart. Fill me with the fruit of joyfulness as I learn to wait upon the Lord. Work in me Your beautiful work of righteousness.

June 26

The "Who" *of* Life

Then Moses said to God, "Indeed, when I come to the children of Israel and say to them, 'The God of your fathers has sent me to you,' and they say to me, 'What is His name?' what shall I say to them?" And God said to Moses, "I AM WHO I AM."

EXODUS 3:13–14 NKJV

Get the "who" of life settled and everything else falls into place. Get the "who" wrong and nothing adds up. The "who" of life is "Him"—the Eternal God, the Creator, the Sustainer of all things, the great I AM.

The "who" of life is also the "wow" of life.

June 27

The "What" *of* Life

He said to them,
When you pray, say:
Father, hallowed be Your name.
Your kingdom come.
LUKE 11:2 AMP

The "what" of life is His will being done in you and through you. Let what He desires for your life be your highest purpose and deepest passion.

JUNE 28

THE "WHERE" *of* LIFE

Teach me to do Your will,
for You are my God.
May Your gracious Spirit lead me
forward on a firm footing.
PSALM 143:10 NLT

The "where" of life is to follow His leading. He wants you to be in His appointed place. It may be a small place or a hidden place, but it is His place for you, and that means it is the best place you can be.

JUNE 29

THE "WHEN" *of* LIFE

He has made everything beautiful in its time.
ECCLESIASTES 3:11 NKJV

The "when" of life is trusting His timing. You do not need to be ahead of Him or dragging behind. Trust His timing, it is always perfect.

June 30

The "Why" *of* Life

Now may the God of peace who brought up our Lord Jesus from the dead, that great Shepherd of the sheep, through the blood of the everlasting covenant, make you complete in every good work to do His will, working in you what is well pleasing in His sight, through Jesus Christ, to whom be glory forever and ever.

HEBREWS 13:20–21 NKJV

The "why" of life is living for His glory. What you do is important, but why you do it is even more important. Let the "why" of your life be to please Him. Do it all for His sake.

July 1

He Is Near

The Lord is close to all who call on Him, yes, to all who call on Him in truth.

PSALM 145:18 NLT

Don't doubt His presence for a single moment. He is the true and faithful God. You can be certain of Him fulfilling His promises. Don't doubt it. Let your heart be quiet with this assurance! He is near you because He cares about you, because He loves you, and because He desires to have fellowship with you.

There will never be a time, a moment, a second when you are without Him. He is with you now; with you tomorrow; with you in the dark times; with you in the hard times; with you in the glad times; with you through all the times of your life—when you are young, when you are old, when you are busy, when you journey, and when you return home.

July 2

Everlasting Love

Yes, I have loved you with an everlasting love; therefore with loving-kindness have I drawn you and continued My faithfulness to you.

JEREMIAH 31:3 AMP

The love of God is truly amazing! It is too deep to fully explore, too high to fully ascend, and too wide to fully get our understanding around, but it can be believed in our hearts, known in our spirits, and proclaimed with our voices.

His love keeps you, protects you, cares for you, and provides for you. Nothing can get a wedge between you and His love—nothing can push it away, nothing can block its flow, nothing can separate you from its presence.

July 3

Sufficiency

The Lord turned to him and said, "Go in this strength of yours and save Israel from the hand of Midian. Have I not sent you?"
JUDGES 6:14 AMP

Success in your journey is never based on your resources, it is based on God's sufficiency.

When God called Gideon to battle, Gideon had nothing to boast about. He had no confidence in his natural ability or resources. He was full of fear and his faith was shaken. Yet God didn't call him a "nobody" but a "mighty warrior." God told Gideon to step out in his weakness, and when Gideon did, he found himself walking in God's strength.

Is God calling you to take a new step of obedience? When God calls you, He sends you; when He sends you He goes with you; when He goes with you, He equips you; when He equips you, you have everything you need.

July 4

Everyday Tips *for* Living

The wise also will hear and increase in learning, and the person of understanding will acquire skill and attain to sound counsel [so that he may be able to steer his course rightly].

PROVERBS 1:5 AMP

1. Don't ever lose heart; God will never give up on you.
2. Never let your heart run out of thankfulness.
3. Don't feel inferior to anyone. God made only one of you.
4. Don't carry around worry, fear, or anxiety. They are the thieves of peace.
5. Hold things loosely. They are temporary.

JULY 5

WHEN YOU NEED HIM MOST

God is able to make all grace abound toward you,
that you, always having all sufficiency in all things,
may have an abundance for every good work.
II CORINTHIANS 9:8 NKJV

His strongest grace
Is for your weakest moment;
His sweetest fellowship
Is for your loneliest journey;
His richest supply
Is for your neediest hour;
His closest embrace
Is for your deepest sorrow;
His brightest light
Is for your darkest day.

July 6

God's Word

The word of God is living and powerful, and sharper than any two-edged sword, piercing even to the division of soul and spirit, and of joints and marrow, and is a discerner of the thoughts and intents of the heart.

HEBREWS 4:12 NKJV

The Word of God was given for us to believe and obey. It is God's love letter to be welcomed into the human heart. It is the final authority through which all other questions and opinions can be settled. It is relevant to our times, our culture, and our lifestyles. There is no word like the Word of God. No wisdom of man can compare to the absolute, eternal, unshakable, righteous truth of the Word of God.

July 7

God's Love Brings Life

We have known and believed the love that God has for us. God is love, and he who abides in love abides in God, and God in him.

I JOHN 4:16 NKJV

He loves you in every season, yet His love is not seasonal. He loves you in every circumstance, yet His love is not circumstantial. He loves you in every mood, yet His love is not moody. He loves you in every condition, yet His love is not conditional.

July 8

Our Pleasure

Now may the God of peace who brought up our Lord Jesus from the dead, that great Shepherd of the sheep, through the blood of the everlasting covenant, make you complete in every good work to do His will, working in you what is well pleasing in His sight, through Jesus Christ, to whom be glory forever and ever. Amen.

HEBREWS 13:20–21 NKJV

Each of us can seek God's favor in all we do, and we can depend upon His power to accomplish what He has called us to do. Our greatest pleasure is to please Him. Our hearts can be fixed on loving what He loves and celebrating the things that He celebrates.

July 9

You Were Made...

Thank You for making me so wonderfully complex! Your workmanship is marvelous—how well I know it.... How precious are your thoughts about me, O God. They cannot be numbered!

PSALM 139:14, 17 NLT

You were made by God. Live in the awe of that wonder.

You were made to know God. Live in the pleasure of that communion.

You were made for God. Live in the light of that calling.

You were made to please God. Live in the delight of that opportunity.

You were made to walk with God. Live in the love of that companionship.

You were made to glorify God. Live in the beauty of that purpose.

You were made to be with God. Live in the hope of that tomorrow.

July 10

The Word *of* God (Part 1)

So then faith comes by hearing, and hearing by the word of God.
ROMANS 10:17 NKJV

The Word of God:

No warrior can dull its blade;

No intellectual can undermine its truth;

No skeptic can lessen its authenticity;

No mocker can weaken its foundations;

No philosopher can outthink its penetrating insight;

No leader can weaken its authority;

No religion can replace its transforming power.

July 11

The Word *of* God (Part 2)

Your words were found, and I ate them, and Your word was to me the joy and rejoicing of my heart; for I am called by Your name, O Lord God of hosts.

JEREMIAH 15:16 NKJV

The Word of God:

The hungry eat it, the weary rest in it, the traveler is guided by it, the humble learn from it, the submissive obey it, the devout love it, the downcast find encouragement in it, the weary find strength in it, the sick are healed by it, and the wise build their lives upon it.

July 12

Overcoming Temptation

Blessed [happy, spiritually prosperous, favored by God] is the man who is steadfast under trial and perseveres when tempted; for when he has passed the test and been approved, he will receive the [victor's] crown of life which the Lord has promised to those who love Him.

JAMES 1:12 AMP

Temptation is not sin. It can be resisted, refused, and rejected. Temptation can lead to sin when we yield to it, but thankfully, we do not have to yield to temptation. Though the voice of temptation may come to you and say, "Do it now!" "Get it now!" "Be it now!" you can choose to declare, "I will wait for God's time." "I will do it God's way." "I will take my God-given place."

The next time you experience temptation your heart can declare, "Father, I love You too much to say yes to this temptation and to do something that would be displeasing to You."

July 13

Crying Out *to the* Lord

I will lift up my eyes to the hills—
from whence comes my help?
My help comes from the Lord,
who made heaven and earth.

PSALM 121:1–2 NKJV

Your prayers can include Scripture promises such as Psalm 121, where God assures you:

Your help comes from Him.

He will not let you fall.

He will watch over you day and night.

He will protect you from evil.

He will guard your coming in and going out.

Basing your *petition* upon Psalm 121, your prayer can be:

Lord, I cry out to You for help. You have promised You will keep me from falling. Watch over me day and night. God, protect me from all evil. Guard me wherever I go and keep Your hand upon me.

July 14

The Importance of Praise

I will lift up my eyes to the hills—
from whence comes my help?
My help comes from the Lord,
who made heaven and earth.
PSALM 121:1–2 NKJV

In times of need and difficulty it is important to offer to God not only your *petitions* but also your prayers of *praise*. Even when things are hard, you can take Psalm 121 and use it as a prayer of praise:

Lord, thank You for being my help in this difficulty. I praise You for watching over my life and for keeping me from falling. Thank You that You never take Your eye off of me, that You protect me from all evil, and that You are the keeper of my soul. Thank You for the comfort I find in knowing You are guarding me wherever I go.

July 15

God Is More *than* Enough!

May you experience the love of Christ, though it is too great to understand fully. Then you will be made complete with all the fullness of life and power that comes from God.

EPHESIANS 3:19 NLT

He is not the God of the "half empty" or "half full" in our lives.

He is the God of the "exceeding abundantly above all we could ask or think."

His will for us is not just "joy" but "great joy";

Not just "peace" but "peace that passes understanding";

Not just "love" but "fullness of love";

Not just to be a conqueror but to be "more than a conqueror."

When He fills our cup, it is overflowing;

When He flows through us, it is as rivers of living waters;

When He meets a need, He does it out of the riches that are in Christ.

July 16

Abounding Grace

God is able to make all grace abound toward you.
II CORINTHIANS 9:8 NKJV

Grace. What a wonderful word! The very sound of it brings health and healing, comfort and reassurance, encouragement and hope. What does this wonderful word mean and not mean?

Grace is not a license to sin. It does not mean He lets us do whatever we please, whenever we please, while assuring us all is well. Grace is not a permission slip that lets us do our own thing or skip out on our responsibilities. Grace is not a free pass that allows us to escape correction.

Grace is God's power to set us free from everything that displeases Him and bring us into all things that are good and holy.

JULY 17

GRACE *upon* GRACE

Grace, mercy, and peace will be with you from God the Father and from the Lord Jesus Christ, the Son of the Father, in truth and love.

II JOHN 1:3 NKJV

Here are some helpful definitions that have been written by others about grace:

Grace is God's Riches At Christ's Expense.

Grace is God's unmerited favor.

Grace is God working in us the will and the desire to do the things that please Him.

Grace is freely receiving from God what we do not deserve.

Grace is God's influence upon us resulting in happiness and thankfulness.

Grace is amazing!

JULY 18

THE RICHES *of* HIS GRACE

That in the coming ages he might show the immeasurable riches of his grace in kindness toward us in Christ Jesus.

EPHESIANS 2:7 ESV

Grace is like the poor finding a vast treasure, the hungry finding a banqueting table, the weak finding limitless strength, the thirsty finding an artesian well, the fearful finding great courage, the lost finding the way back home, the empty heart finding a reservoir of never-ending love.

JULY 19

GRACE IS *in* CHRIST

Grace and truth came by Jesus Christ.
JOHN 1:17 KJV

God's grace means this: Jesus Christ will *be* to me all that I cannot be; He will *do* for me all that I cannot do; He will work *through* me all He calls me to be. He will give His grace, not in tiny measure, but in overflowing abundance.

July 20

God Orders Your Steps

Let your light so shine before men, that they may see your good works and glorify your Father in heaven.

MATTHEW 5:16 NKJV

Each day we can respond to the opportunities God places before us. Not the opportunities to be famous, powerful, or rich, but the opportunities to glorify Him. These opportunities will often be found amidst the ordinary days and routine moments of our lives.

Today God may give you the opportunity to manifest an attitude that reflects what He thinks and feels; to perform an action that expresses what He wants to do in a certain situation; to share words that speak His heart and His truth into someone's life; or to respond with a kindness that extends His grace and mercy to someone in need.

July 21

Prayer *of* Comfort

You keep track of all my sorrows. You have collected all my tears in Your bottle. You have recorded each one in Your book.

PSALM 56:8 NLT

Through the tears, O God, I bring my hurting heart to You. I cry out with all that is within me to You, the One who is my comfort and my Comforter. You know my weeping, You see my sorrow, You hear my cry. My tears drop upon the pages of Your book that hold the promises of hope and comfort that You have written for me to lean upon. Thank You that You have drawn close to me to gather my tears and keep them in Your bottle, to assure me that You will not forget about me or be indifferent to what I am going through.

JULY 22

PATIENCE

Strengthened with all might, according to His glorious power, unto all patience and longsuffering with joyfulness.
COLOSSIANS 1:11 KJV

Patience is the result of a life that is submitted to God's will. We become impatient when we replace God's timetable with our own. God doesn't need to hurry up or catch up, because His timing is always perfect. When we become impatient we want to make things fit into our own schedule. This can quickly open the door to anger and frustration.

Patience and contentment are very closely related. While contentment frees us from murmuring and complaining, patience frees us from fretting and striving. A contented heart will bring forth thankfulness, and a patient heart will bring forth calmness. You will have a quiet heart when contentment and patience are abiding within.

July 23

Patience Is *the* Holy Spirit's Fruit

In purity and sincerity, in knowledge and spiritual insight, in patience, in kindness, in the Holy Spirit, in genuine love.

II CORINTHIANS 6:6 AMP

The patience of the Holy Spirit does not produce heaviness or frustration but joyfulness. The patience of the Holy Spirit frees us from the strife of wanting things to go our way, according to our clock and calendar. Patience is a peaceable fruit of righteousness and is a beautiful work of the Spirit when we see it operating within us and in the lives of others. Today, let the music of the Holy Spirit sing out in your heart, "In Your time, Lord, make all things beautiful."

July 24

Jesus Is *the* Way (Part 1)

I am the way.

JOHN 14:6 NLT

By the blood of Jesus, **come.** Hebrews 10:19–20

By the invitation of Jesus, **follow.** Mark 1:17

From the grace of Jesus, **receive.** John 1:14

On the foundation of Jesus, **build.** I Corinthians 3:11

Through the power of Jesus, **serve.** Acts 1:8

In the righteousness of Jesus, **stand.** Philippians 3:9

July 25

Jesus Is *the* Way (Part 2)

I am the way.
JOHN 14:6 NLT

In the life of Jesus, **thrive.** John 10:10

In the words of Jesus, **trust.** John 6:63

In the authority of Jesus, **obey.** Matthew 28:18–19

In the resurrection of Jesus, **hope.** John 14:19

In the peace of Jesus, **rest.** John 14:27

In the love of Jesus, **abide.** Ephesians 3:17–19

July 26

Prayer *for the* Day

Now may the God of peace who brought up our Lord Jesus from the dead, that great Shepherd of the sheep, through the blood of the everlasting covenant, make you complete in every good work to do His will, working in you what is well pleasing in His sight, through Jesus Christ, to whom be glory forever and ever. Amen.

HEBREWS 13:20–21 NKJV

Father, through my face may Your light shine;
Through my voice may Your praise be heard;
Through my hands may Your works be extended;
Through my life may Your grace abound;
Through my heart may Your love be given away.

JULY 27

TRUSTING *the* LORD

Trust in Him at all times, you people; pour out your heart before Him; God is a refuge for us. Selah.

PSALM 62:8 NKJV

Each day you can put your trust in the Lord. You can take all your cares, fears, and worries out of your hands and place them into His hands. You can trust Him because He is with you and will never fail.

In your needs trust Him for His provision.

In your difficulties trust Him for His solution.

In your uncertainties trust Him for His wisdom.

In your tears trust Him for His comfort.

In your struggles trust Him for His peace.

July 28

Prayer *for* Guidance

Trust in the Lord with all your heart; do not depend on your own understanding.

PROVERBS 3:5 NLT

Heavenly Father, You have promised to guide me, instruct me, and direct my steps. I need to hear Your voice, know Your will, sense Your guidance. I acknowledge You as the One who is wholly and uniquely able and qualified to lead and direct my life. I thank You that You have not asked me to try and figure everything out, to trust in my own reasoning, or to rely upon my understanding of what is best for me.

Father, I receive Your wisdom, knowing that every decision You make is the right decision and the one that is always the best that can be made. You do all things well! I trust in Your timing to bring into my life the right things at the right time.

July 29

Looking *unto* Jesus

Looking unto Jesus the author and finisher of our faith.
HEBREWS 12:2 KJV

The hymn writer Clara T. Williams boldly proclaimed, "Hallelujah! I have found Him who my soul so long has craved!"

Our search for meaning, for purpose, for forgiveness, for hope, for peace, and for life itself is over because we have found our Savior, our Redeemer, our Healer, our King, and our Friend.

He is with you, He is in you, and He has promised never to leave nor forsake you.

July 30

How *to* See Jesus

Jesus said to him, "Because you have seen Me, do you now believe? Blessed [happy, spiritually secure, and favored by God] are they who did not see [Me] and yet believed [in Me]."

JOHN 20:29 AMP

God chose not to give us a detailed physical description of Jesus in the Scriptures. One thing God does tell us is found in Isaiah 53:2 (NLT): "There was nothing beautiful or majestic about His appearance, nothing to attract us to Him."

But the truth is, we don't need to have a physical image of Jesus to believe in Him.

We see Him now with the eyes of faith. What we see with our spiritual eyes is enough to satisfy. One day we will see Him as He is and know Him as we are known.

July 31

Eyes *of* Faith

Keep yourselves in the love of God, looking for the mercy of our Lord Jesus Christ unto eternal life.

JUDE 1:21 NKJV

Look to Jesus with...

A look of *dependence.*

A look of *confidence.*

A look of *assurance.*

Look to Jesus as your sufficiency, your authority, and your coming King.

August 1

Trust *in the* Lord (Part 1)

As for God, His way is perfect; the word of the Lord *is proven; He is a shield to all who trust in Him.*

PSALM 18:30 NKJV

One of the best things you can do today is to trust in the Lord. To fully trust Him means to release all the things that concern you and place them into His hands.

Here are three important questions you can ask yourself as you go through your day: Am I taking this action, thinking these thoughts, or speaking these words as an expression of my trust in the Lord?

AUGUST 2

TRUST IN THE LORD (PART 2)

Trust in Him at all times, you people; pour out your heart before Him; God is a refuge for us. Selah.

PSALM 62:8 NKJV

Trust in the Lord, not for something, but for everything; not in a few things, but in all things; not sometime, but at all times.

Do you have a problem? Trust Him for His solution.

Do you have a need? Trust Him for His provision.

Do you have a question? Trust Him for His answer.

August 3

Trust *in the* Lord (Part 3)

Trust in the Lord with all your heart; do not depend on your own understanding. Seek His will in all you do, and He will show you which path to take.

PROVERBS 3:5–6 NLT

You can trust in the Lord with all your heart and hold nothing back because He is the God of the "always has been" and He is the God of the "never will be."

He has always been true and He has never been deceptive.

He has always been faithful and He has never been forgetful.

He has always been wise and He has never been imprudent.

He has always been all-knowing and He has never been unaware.

He has always been loving and He has never been unkind.

He has always been good and He has never been unrighteous.

August 4

God's Guidance

What is that to you? As for you, follow Me.
JOHN 21:22 NLT

You can know what God is asking you to do and not be led astray by what others think you should do. As the Holy Spirit guides you, He will not say yes to every opportunity that presents itself to you. Not every interest is God's will for you. Don't be hesitant if the Holy Spirit is directing you in a different way from others. What He is telling others may not be what He has for you. Walk in His peace, follow God's chosen path, and take your God-given place.

August 5

Work Out

God is working in you, giving you the desire and the power to do what pleases Him.

PHILIPPIANS 2:13 NLT

Reach out in prayer;

Step out in faithful obedience;

Move out in His grace and mercy;

Give out all He has freely given you;

Speak out His words of life and hope;

Live out what He is working within you;

Keep out all that is displeasing in His sight;

Cast out every fear and bondage of the enemy;

Pour out a sacrifice of thanksgiving and praise.

August 6

God Is Great

Great is the Lord, and greatly to be praised.
PSALM 48:1 KJV

God is great. He has no competition.

No one will ever out give Him, outsmart Him, or outthink Him.

No one will ever take away His crown or dethrone Him. God's greatness will never fade; it will never be weakened or diminish. God will never lose His greatness, and He will never go into retirement.

But God, who is rich in mercy, because of His great love with which He loved us, even when we were dead in trespasses, made us alive together with Christ (by grace you have been saved), and raised us up together, and made us sit together in the heavenly places in Christ Jesus, that in the ages to come He might show the exceeding riches of His grace in His kindness toward us in Christ Jesus. Ephesians 2:4–7 NKJV

August 7

God's Love Is Great

Behold, a woman in the city who was a sinner, when she knew that Jesus sat at the table in the Pharisee's house, brought an alabaster flask of fragrant oil, and stood at His feet behind Him weeping; and she began to wash His feet with her tears, and wiped them with the hair of her head; and she kissed His feet and anointed them with the fragrant oil.

LUKE 7:37–38 NKJV

God loves you more than anyone could ever love you. You can pour out upon Him your praise, worship, and thankfulness. There is no reason to hold anything back. This type of devotion is beautifully demonstrated by the account of the woman who poured her alabaster box of fragrant oil upon the feet of Jesus. Like her, you can pour out upon Him your greatest and deepest heartfelt devotion.

August 8

Blessed

On that day [when that time comes] you will know for yourselves that I am in My Father, and you are in Me, and I am in you.

JOHN 14:20 AMP

God blesses you with all spiritual blessings. You are blessed with the things that last forever. They come to you from heaven and are placed within your heart. They are yours because you are in Christ. No measure of mercy is missing, no portion of peace is withheld. Through these spiritual blessings Jesus is saying to you, "I am giving you My heart…its holiness, its goodness, its loveliness. Live in Me as I live in you."

August 9

How It Happens

Unfailing love and truth have met together.
Righteousness and peace have kissed!
PSALM 85:10 NLT

Righteousness is how peace happens. Psalm 85:10

Truth is how freedom happens. John 8:32

Grace is how strength happens. II Corinthians 12:9

Abiding is how fruit happens. John 15:4

Trust is how guidance happens. Proverbs 3:5–6

Prayer is how receiving happens. Matthew 7:7

Love is how obedience happens. John 14:15

Holiness is how beauty happens. I Chronicles 16:29

Faith is how pleasing God happens. Hebrews 11:6

Jesus is how it all happens! Colossians 1:16–17

August 10

Road Noise

Let me hear what God the Lord will speak,
for he will speak peace to his people.
PSALM 85:8 ESV

In many ways, life creates a lot of "road noise" for us. The clamor of life can get louder as our pace gets faster, as our schedules become more hectic, as our days get busier, and as our circumstances get tougher. These "road noises" of life can create confusion, frustration, anxiety, and stress if left unchecked.

Is the pace of your life creating a high level of "road noise"? Is the sound of His still small voice barely discernible? If so, it is time to quiet your heart. It is time to "be still and know that He is God." It is time to wait upon the Lord and have your strength renewed. It is time to hear Him say to you, "Peace, be still!"

AUGUST 11

GOD IS GOOD

No one is good but One, that is, God.
MATTHEW 19:17 NKJV

Because God is good, everything that comes to you from Him is meant for your benefit. God's good is the highest good! The Gospel is the "Good News" because it comes to us from God. We are also assured that He will not withhold any good thing from those who walk uprightly before Him.

We are told in the Scriptures that God is able to work all things together for good for those who love Him and are called according to His purpose. In ways that you may not fully know or understand, God is able to take even the hard and difficult things you go through and use them for the good.

Goodness, not evil, will always have the final say in your life as you trust God to fulfill His purposes for you.

August 12

God Is Always Working *for the* Good

As for you, you meant evil against me; but God meant it for good, in order to bring it about as it is this day, to save many people alive.

GENESIS 50:20 NKJV

After years of hardship, unfairness, rejection, and isolation, Joseph was able to recognize that God meant all of it for good.

Joseph understood the goodness of God because he was able to witness the purpose of God fulfilled through all he experienced. The good purpose of God was something much greater than just the life and well-being of Joseph, it was to save the lives of the children of Israel.

Your life is not just about God being good to you, but also about God using you to extend His goodness to others today.

August 13

God's Goodness Is Following You

Surely goodness and mercy shall follow me all the days of my life; and I will dwell in the house of the LORD forever.

PSALM 23:6 NKJV

Whatever you may be going through today, no matter how dark the sky appears or how deep the valley takes you, be assured that God has not abandoned you. And because He is with you, goodness has not abandoned you…it will follow you all the days of your life, and goodness will prevail.

August 14

Living Water

Jesus answered and said to her, "If you knew the gift of God, and who it is who says to you, 'Give Me a drink,' you would have asked Him, and He would have given you living water."

JOHN 4:10 NKJV

The well that the woman of Samaria drew from had natural water;

Jesus' well has Living Water.

Natural water comes from hydrogen and oxygen;

Living Water comes from the Holy Spirit.

Natural water meets a physical need;

Living Water meets a spiritual need.

To have water from a well you work hard and dig deep before you come to it;

To have Living Water you rest and the Holy Spirit comes to you.

August 15

Walking *in the* Spirit

If we live in the Spirit, let us also walk in the Spirit.
GALATIANS 5:25 KJV

What a privilege you have today to walk as Jesus walked. Jesus spent each day dependent upon the Holy Spirit's presence. Jesus was led by the Holy Spirit and did His Father's will through the power of the Holy Spirit.

You can walk as Jesus walked because Jesus sent the Holy Spirit to be with you, to live in you, to come upon you, and to fill you. The Holy Spirit will teach you, guide you, lead you, and equip you to walk in the ways that magnify Jesus and please the Father.

August 16

Walking *by* Faith

If we live in the Spirit, let us also walk in the Spirit.
GALATIANS 5:25 NKJV

When you walk in the strength of the Spirit you will…

Walk by faith. *For we walk by faith, not by sight. II Corinthians 5:7 NKJV*

Walk in love. *Walk in love, as Christ also hath loved us, and hath given Himself for us an offering and a sacrifice to God for a sweetsmelling savour. Ephesians 5:2 KJV*

Walk in the light. *If we say that we have fellowship with Him, and walk in darkness, we lie, and do not the truth: but if we walk in the light, as He is in the light, we have fellowship one with another, and the blood of Jesus Christ His Son cleanseth us from all sin. I John 1:6–7 KJV*

August 17

Walking *in the* Truth

I rejoiced greatly that I have found some of your children walking in truth, as we received commandment from the Father.

II JOHN 1:4 NKJV

When you walk in the strength of the Spirit you will…

Walk in truth. *I have no greater joy than to hear that my children walk in truth. III John 1:4 NKJV*

Walk in a worthy manner. *That you would walk worthy of God who calls you into His own kingdom and glory. I Thessalonians 2:12 NKJV*

Walk wisely. *Walk in wisdom toward them that are without, redeeming the time. Colossians 4:5 KJV*

Walk properly. *Let us walk properly, as in the day, not in revelry and drunkenness, not in lewdness and lust, not in strife and envy. Romans 13:13 NKJV*

August 18

Jesus Calls You

Take My yoke upon you and learn from Me.
MATTHEW 11:29 NKJV

I speak to you the promises that come from My Father's heart.

Trust in Me.

I place My hands over you and pour out My richest blessings upon you.

Receive from Me.

I wait for you with outstretched arms to assure you of My love.

Run to Me.

I am your song, I want to fill your heart with My praises.

Delight in Me.

August 19

Jesus Calls You

Look! I stand at the door and knock. If you hear my voice and open the door, I will come in, and we will share a meal together as friends.
REVELATION 3:20 NLT

Don't be foolish or slow of heart, I will not pass you by.

Sit with Me.

I am your healer, the restorer of your soul, and the One who forgives.

Turn to Me.

I will lead you to still waters and quiet resting places.

Walk with Me.

Let My words be as a flame of love that burns deep within you.

Sup with Me.

Why are you troubled and why do doubts arise so easily?

Look to Me.

August 20

Jesus Calls You

Then Jesus said to those Jews who believed Him, "If you abide in My word, you are My disciples indeed."

JOHN 8:31 NKJV

What I have told you I am faithful to fulfill.

Rest in Me.

Let Me open your understanding so you can know all I have done for you.

Learn of Me.

I am glorified and have sent you the promise of My Father.

Drink of Me.

I will be your source of joy and fruitfulness. You will never be empty.

Abide in Me.

August 21

In His Hands

My Father, who has given them to Me,
is greater than all; and no one is able to
snatch them out of My Father's hand.

JOHN 10:29 NKJV

Into whose hands can we place our lives? Many have taken the risk of placing their lives into the hands of someone they trusted, only to have that person fail them and leave their lives broken. When someone we've trusted fails us, it can be hard to trust again.

It is God alone who calls you to place your life fully in His hands. He cannot fail. How awesome are God's hands! His hands formed the heavens, touched and cured the leper, opened the eyes of the blind, blessed the children, lifted the lame, washed the disciples' feet, broke bread, and fed a multitude.

It is in God's hands alone that you will be kept, cared for, and protected.

August 22

His Life Is Your Life

For to me to live is Christ.
PHILIPPIANS 1:21 ESV

Jesus Christ is an undefeated Savior! His death on the cross was not a defeat but a victory. He defeated sin, death, and Satan. Jesus Christ has never faced an enemy and lost. Jesus Christ faced temptation. He was despised and rejected. He went through great suffering, yet He was never defeated.

Jesus Christ walked among us, died on the cross, rose from the grave, ascended to heaven, and now sits at the right hand of God, undefeated. We, who have known defeated lives, can now know His victory. As a believer in Jesus Christ, His life is your life.

August 23

His Strength Is Your Strength

But thanks be to God, who gives us the victory [as conquerors] through our Lord Jesus Christ.

I CORINTHIANS 15:57 AMP

Are you facing hardship or difficulty, temptation or opposition, disappointment or discouragement? Let Jesus be your victory—let His strength be your strength, let His endurance be your endurance, let His peace be your peace. Place no confidence in what you can do, but place all your trust in what He can do. Let Him keep you through every storm.

Let this simple prayer be in your heart and upon your lips today, "Jesus, live Your undefeated life in me today."

August 24

God Loves You *in* Christ

God showed His great love for us by sending Christ to die for us while we were still sinners.
ROMANS 5:8 NLT

As a believer, the truth that God loves you is something you need to hear often. One of the reasons is because the enemy spends so much time telling you that God doesn't love you. God wants you to both *know* and *believe* the love that He has for you. *Behold, what manner of love the Father hath bestowed upon us, that we should be called the sons of God. I John 3:1 KJV.*

August 25

God Loves You Forever *in* Christ

Christ Jesus died for us and was raised to life for us, and He is sitting in the place of honor at God's right hand, pleading for us. Can anything ever separate us from Christ's love?

ROMANS 8:34–35 NLT

Be assured of His love. Rest in His love. Be renewed in His love. Christ came for you. Christ died for you. Christ lives for you. You are greatly loved. This is the good news of the Gospel. This is your good news.

Where will this great love take you? What will it mean to you today and for all your tomorrows?

August 26

Knowing God's Love

The Lord has appeared of old to me, saying:
"Yes, I have loved you with an everlasting love;
therefore with lovingkindness I have drawn you."
JEREMIAH 31:3 NKJV

Let the Holy Spirit begin to sweep over your soul and reveal to you the greatness, the fullness, and the completeness of God's love. Ask Him to open your eyes to see and your heart to know the love of God in ways you have never known or thought possible. And what He shows you, believe it to be so.

August 27

Keep *on* Asking

Call unto Me, and I will answer thee, and show thee great and mighty things, which thou knowest not.

JEREMIAH 33:3 KJV

The great and mighty things that God wants to show you are often the answers to prayers that you have prayed. Keep on asking, keep on seeking, keep on knocking—answers will come, doors will be opened, promises will be fulfilled. Take heart...He is working on the behalf of those who wait for Him.

AUGUST 28

PRAYER *of* HOPE

So be strong and courageous, all you who put your hope in the LORD!
PSALM 31:24 NLT

Father, thank You for being the God of hope and my hope. You alone are the source and the reason for my hope. Because of You, I can pray in hope; walk in hope; believe in hope; endure in hope; overcome in hope; live in hope.

When I look to the future I have hope because You are already in the future. Father, it is Your hope that frees from the despair of hopelessness and the insecurity of false hope.

When I look ahead, I do not see the details clearly, but I see You, the One who is in all the details of what is ahead. I believe in Your plan and purpose for my life.

August 29

Even Though (Part 1)

My thoughts are not your thoughts, neither are your ways My ways, says the Lord.

ISAIAH 55:8 AMP

Trust His ways, even though they may not be your ways.

Take His hand, even though it means letting go of what you are hanging onto.

Depend upon His strength, even though you are aware of your weakness.

Please His heart, even though it may mean not having the approval of others.

August 30

Even Though (Part 2)

Trust in the Lord with all your heart, and lean not on your own understanding; in all your ways acknowledge Him, and He shall direct your paths.

PROVERBS 3:5–6 NKJV

Obey His Word, even though you hear different opinions.

Follow His path, even though it may take you through valleys and hills.

Seek His wisdom, even though you don't understand everything He's doing.

Rest in His love, even though you may be tempted to worry or fear.

August 31

The Lord Has *the* Final Say

The thief's purpose is to steal and kill and destroy. My purpose is to give them a rich and satisfying life.

JOHN 10:10 NLT

You belong to God, my dear children. You have already won a victory…because the Spirit who lives in you is greater than the spirit who lives in the world.

I JOHN 4:4 NLT

You are the Lord's and He *has* the final say. You are the Lord's and He *is* the final authority. No scheme of the enemy and no plan of man need take from you what Jesus came to give to you, to be to you, and to work through you.

SEPTEMBER 1

A PRAYER *to* YOUR SHEPHERD (PART 1)

A hired hand will run when he sees a wolf coming. He will abandon the sheep because they don't belong to him and he isn't their shepherd. And so the wolf attacks them and scatters the flock.

JOHN 10:12 NLT

Jesus,

Your arms are open.

Your heart welcomes me—

I run to You because

You do not run away from me.

You are present—

In the hardest moment.

In the deepest trial.

In the greatest test.

No matter what I am facing,

You are here because You care.

SEPTEMBER 2

A PRAYER *to* YOUR SHEPHERD (PART 2)

I am the good shepherd. The good shepherd gives His life for the sheep.
JOHN 10:11 NKJV

Jesus,

You gave Your life for me.

You opened the door

Into every good and perfect gift.

You are my good day.

My good night.

My good way.

My soul breathes the air of Your goodness—

And I am comforted.

September 3

A Prayer *to* Your Shepherd (Part 3)

Yet they will by no means follow a stranger, but will flee from him, for they do not know the voice of strangers.

JOHN 10:5 NKJV

Jesus,

Thank You for being here.

When I flee from strangers,

I flee to You.

You welcome me.

You receive me.

You are my secure place.

In Your presence

I am always safe—

I am always home.

SEPTEMBER 4

A PRAYER *to* YOUR SHEPHERD (PART 4)

He calls his own sheep by name.

JOHN 10:3 NKJV

esus,

You know me.

You know everything about me.

You get me.

You made me.

You bought me.

You love me.

I am so happy

To know You know my name!

SEPTEMBER 5

A PRAYER *to* YOUR SHEPHERD (PART 5)

I am the door. If anyone enters by Me, he will be saved, and will go in and out and find pasture.
JOHN 10:9 NKJV

Jesus,

I love Your presence.

You are the door into each new day.

You don't lead me around in circles,

Or lead about in confusion.

I trust in Your wisdom—

In Your path,

In Your plan,

In Your purpose,

In Your place for me today.

SEPTEMBER 6

A PRAYER *to* YOUR SHEPHERD (PART 6)

Most assuredly, I say to you, he who does not enter the sheepfold by the door, but climbs up some other way, the same is a thief and a robber. But he who enters by the door is the shepherd of the sheep.

JOHN 10:1–2 NKJV

Jesus,

Thank You for Your sheepfold.

It is a place of protection,

And a safe place for me.

Thank You for entering

By the door of the sheepfold—

You never sneak up on me,

You will never cause me to be fearful,

And I know You will never do me any harm.

September 7

A Prayer *to* Your Shepherd (Part 7)

To him the doorkeeper opens, and the sheep hear his voice; and he calls his own sheep by name and leads them out.

John 10:3 NKJV

Jesus,

My ear is turned toward You.

I am listening.

I love the sound of Your voice.

You call to me because You know me—

I am so thankful that no sheep of Yours

Will ever hear You say,

"You are on your own."

September 8

A Prayer *to* Your Shepherd (Part 8)

If a man has a hundred sheep and one of them gets lost, what will he do? Won't he leave the ninety-nine others in the wilderness and go to search for the one that is lost until he finds it? And when he has found it, he will joyfully carry it home on his shoulders.

LUKE 15:4–5 NLT

*esus,*

Thank You that when You counted Your sheep

You knew that I was missing.

Thank You that You knew where I had wandered,

Came after me…and carried me back.

It is so good to be with You—

Home, in Your fold, where I belong!

September 9

A Prayer *to* Your Shepherd (Part 9)

When he brings out his own sheep, he goes before them; and the sheep follow him, for they know his voice.

JOHN 10:4 NKJV

Jesus,

You are a speaking Shepherd.

I love the sound of Your voice.

I love Your words.

I love Your tone.

I love the things I hear

That come from Your heart.

I am listening.

I am ready to follow.

September 10

A Prayer *to* Your Shepherd (Part 10)

The Lord is my shepherd.

PSALM 23:1 NLT

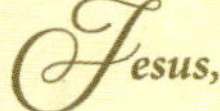esus,

Your name is Lord.

You are in control…

When I try to be,

Things can quickly unravel.

Thank You for the security that comes

When I take things out of my hands

And place them into Yours.

You do all things well!

September 11

A Prayer *to* Your Shepherd (Part 11)

I shall not want.

Psalm 23:1 NKJV

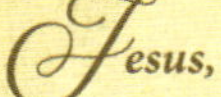

It's a new day.

I don't know what all my needs will be.

But You do!

I am confident that at day's end,

I will look back and say,

"Nothing I needed was missing because I had You!"

SEPTEMBER 12

A PRAYER *to* YOUR SHEPHERD (PART 12)

He makes me to lie down in green pastures.

PSALM 23:2 NKJV

*esus,*

Thank You for feeding me.

I've never

Followed You anywhere

And been empty.

Even if I were in a desert place,

I know I would find Your stream,

And it would bring me to a flourishing place.

SEPTEMBER 13

A PRAYER *to* YOUR SHEPHERD (PART 13)

He leads me beside the still waters.
PSALM 23:2 NKJV

esus,

You lead me

Beside still waters.

You are Peace.

You give peace.

I have peace,

Because I have You.

SEPTEMBER 14

A PRAYER *to* YOUR SHEPHERD (PART 14)

He restores my soul.

PSALM 23:3 NKJV

Jesus,

We are on a steep climb today.

Thank You for the resting places

You prepare along the way.

In these quiet moments,

As I wait upon You,

Restore my soul.

SEPTEMBER 15

A PRAYER *to* YOUR SHEPHERD (PART 15)

He leads me.

PSALM 23:3 NKJV

Jesus,

Thank You

For making guidance

An uncomplicated thing

For me to understand.

You are the Guide.

I follow You.

I am guided.

SEPTEMBER 16

A PRAYER *to* YOUR SHEPHERD (PART 16)

He leads me in the paths of righteousness for His name's sake.
PSALM 23:3 NKJV

Jesus,

Thank You for the right path.

The right way.

The right time.

The right place.

The right reason.

The right response.

There is nothing wrong

About anything You are doing in my life.

SEPTEMBER 17

A PRAYER *to* YOUR SHEPHERD (PART 17)

Your rod and Your staff, they comfort me.

PSALM 23:4 NKJV

*esus,*

Thank You for being my Comfort!

You are so personal.

So near.

So real.

So good.

You never forget about me.

Never! Not for one second.

September 18

The Shepherd (Part 1)

Please listen, O Shepherd of Israel, you who lead Joseph's descendants like a flock. O God, enthroned above the cherubim, display Your radiant glory.

PSALM 80:1 NLT

Find me, Shepherd, as You seek
Your lost and wandering lamb.
Hold me, Shepherd, when You come—
Trembling as I am.

Carry me, Shepherd, with the care
That I'm so needful of—
Keep me close beside Your heart,
Safe within Your love.

SEPTEMBER 19

THE SHEPHERD (PART 2)

The LORD is my Shepherd [to feed, to guide and to shield me], I shall not want.

PSALM 23:1 AMP

Guide me, Shepherd, in the way
That leads to waters still—
May I feed in quietness
Within Your perfect will.

Seeker, Healer, Keeper,
Guardian of my way,
Holder of the rod and staff
That comforts me today.

September 20

Thankfulness (Part 1)

Be thankful in all circumstances, for this is God's will for you who belong to Christ Jesus.
I THESSALONIANS 5:18 NLT

Give thanks *in* everything. (I Thessalonians 5:18)

Give thanks *for* everything. (Ephesians 5:20)

Pray about everything *with* thanksgiving. (Philippians 4:6)

Do all things *without* murmuring. (Philippians 2:14)

Thankfulness is the presence of gratitude and the absence of murmuring.

Thankfulness is an attitude of appreciation for everything that is received; murmuring is an attitude of complaint for everything that is withheld.

Thankfulness is rooted in humility; murmuring is rooted in pride.

September 21

Thankfulness (Part 2)

Shout with joy to the Lord, all the earth! Worship the Lord with gladness. Come before Him, singing with joy. Acknowledge that the Lord is God! He made us, and we are His. We are His people, the sheep of His pasture. Enter His gates with thanksgiving; go into His courts with praise. Give thanks to Him and praise His name. For the Lord is good. His unfailing love continues forever, and His faithfulness continues to each generation.

PSALM 100 NLT

Thankfulness says, "This is more than I deserve"; murmuring says, "I deserve more!"

Thankfulness is the doorway to contentment; murmuring is the doorway to dissatisfaction.

Thankfulness travels on the highway of joy; murmuring travels on the highway of gloom.

Thankfulness causes the disposition to be sweet; murmuring causes the disposition to become sour.

SEPTEMBER 22

INTO *the* DARKNESS...

In Him was life, and the life was the light of
men. And the light shines in the darkness,
and the darkness did not comprehend it.
JOHN 1:4–5 NKJV

Into our darkness came God's purest Light;
Into our sin came God's perfect Savior;
Into our wandering came God's caring Shepherd;
Into our uncertainty came God's sure Foundation;
Into our sadness came God's fullest Joy;
Into our hunger came God's broken Bread;
Into our sickness came God's healing Fountain;
Into our sorrow came God's tender Comfort;
Into our heaviness came God's eternal Song;
Into our restlessness came God's quieting Peace;
Into our loneliness came God's truest Friend;
Into our fear came God's redeeming Love.

September 23

When You Sense Him Most

Blessed [gratefully praised and adored] be the God and Father of our Lord Jesus Christ, the Father of mercies and the God of all comfort, who comforts and encourages us in every trouble so that we will be able to comfort and encourage those who are in any kind of trouble, with the comfort with which we ourselves are comforted by God.

II CORINTHIANS 1:3–4 AMP

It is often in the hardest place that we hear God's softest voice; in the weakest moment that we find His greatest strength; in the loneliest hour that we sense His closest companionship; in the deepest sorrow that we feel His gentlest touch; in the darkest time that we see His brightest light; in the harshest rejection that we know His most reassuring embrace.

September 24

God Truly Loves You

We know how dearly God loves us,
because He has given us the Holy Spirit
to fill our hearts with His love.
ROMANS 5:5 NLT

Knowing the love of God in your life is not guesswork but a reality that is imparted to you by the person of the Holy Spirit.

What a beautiful work the Holy Spirit does in you as He fills your heart with divine love and draws you to the heart of the Father.

September 25

Benediction

Your road led through the sea, your pathway through the mighty waters—a pathway no one knew was there!

PSALM 77:19 NLT

May you set your sail of faith to capture the trade winds of the Spirit's moving. May He carry you into the strong currents of God's grace, to the harbors of Jesus' comfort, to the ports that abound with blessings, and to the warm waters of the Father's love.

May the Captain of your salvation pilot you through troubled seas, quieting your heart when rolling waves beat against you. May you daily be kept from drifting away from the course He has set for you. May He guide you to safe havens, fill your vessel with eternal treasures, and bring you triumphantly to heaven's distant shore.

September 26

May You Find Christ *to* Be...

I can do all things [which He has called me to do] through Him who strengthens and empowers me [to fulfill His purpose—I am self-sufficient in Christ's sufficiency.

PHILIPPIANS 4:13 AMP

The peace for every struggle,
The supply for every need,
The escape for every temptation,
The release for every burden,
The balm for every pain,
The comfort for every sorrow,
The victory for every battle,
The wisdom for every decision,
The strength for every endeavor,
The hope for every tomorrow,
The song for every day.

SEPTEMBER 27

GOD'S PERFECT WAY

My times are in Your hands.
PSALM 31:15 AMP

My steps, my times, my plans, Lord, are daily in Your hands—

As a yielded servant, I wait on Your command.

I want to seek Your kingdom and have You reign in me—

So I can live before You, as one who's been set free.

I cast my cares upon You and trust You for each day—

I want the course You planned for me to be what I obey.

I have no expectations, there only is Your will—

No need to strive or worry, I need only to be still.

SEPTEMBER 28

THE SOUND *of* HIS VOICE

His mouth is full of sweetness; Yes, he is altogether lovely and desirable. This is my beloved and this is my friend, O daughters of Jerusalem.

SONG OF SOLOMON 5:16 AMP

Jesus' voice brings the sweetest sound, the deepest love, the wisest words, the surest way, the greatest comfort, and the fullest life.

It is better to hear His voice than the voice of strangers, better to know His guidance than to be led astray, better to know His counsel than follow wrong opinions; better to believe His truth than the lies of the enemy.

Jesus said that His sheep hear His voice. If you hear a voice you do not recognize, do not respond. Wrong voices take you to wrong places. It is through Jesus' words that you will know His will, His ways, and His heart.

SEPTEMBER 29

GAIN WHAT YOU CANNOT LOSE

What will it profit a man if he gains the whole world, and loses his own soul? Or what will a man give in exchange for his soul?

MARK 8:36–37 NKJV

This question causes us to weigh what is temporal against what is eternal; what rusts and fades away compared to what lasts forever. This question will help you put everything in your life into its proper place—whether your material possessions are great or small, you will lose them one day. The riches you have in Jesus will only deepen and grow greater, without decay or loss. The person without Jesus will miss it all; the person who has Jesus will lack nothing and will have a part in the best that is yet to be.

September 30

If

Peace I leave with you, My peace I give to you; not as the world gives do I give to you. Let not your heart be troubled, neither let it be afraid.

JOHN 14:27 NKJV

If Jesus is who He said He is;

If Jesus can do all He said He can do;

If Jesus will come like He said He would come;

If Jesus loves you like He said He loves you;

You have no reason to be afraid or troubled,

And every reason to be at peace.

October 1

Be Full *of* Hope

Looking for the blessed hope and glorious appearing of our great God and Savior Jesus Christ.
TITUS 2:13 NKJV

In Titus 2:13 we are reminded that as believers we are to live in hope. Our hope is so great and so sure that the Scriptures call our hope the "blessed hope." What is this blessed hope? It is the glorious appearing of our great God and Savior, Jesus Christ! Think of it: as a believer, you will see Jesus, not as your judge to condemn you but as your Savior to receive you when He comes again.

October 2

Nothing Is...

Great is the Lord, and greatly to be praised;
and His greatness is unsearchable.
PSALM 145:3 NKJV

You are seated with Christ at God's right hand...

Nothing is higher than that!

God loves you with an everlasting love...

Nothing is deeper than that!

He invites you to drink from the river of His delights...

Nothing is purer than that!

He shares His heart with you in communion...

Nothing is dearer than that!

He watches over you with tender mercies...

Nothing is kinder than that!

October 3

Nothing Is...

I know that the Lord is great and
that our Lord is above all gods.
PSALM 135:5 AMP

He upholds you within the grip of His right hand…

Nothing is stronger than that!

He leads you according to the counsel of His own will…

Nothing is wiser than that!

He faithfully feeds you from His Word…

Nothing is truer than that!

He is with you and will never leave you…

Nothing is nearer than that!

He is in you and joined to your spirit…

Nothing is closer than that!

OCTOBER 4

SIMPLICITY *and* WONDER

I assure you and most solemnly say to you, whoever does not receive and welcome the kingdom of God like a child will not enter it at all.

MARK 10:15 AMP

Walk with God as a child. Never lose the simplicity of trust and the world of wonder that a child lives in from day to day. Walk with your eyes on your Father—happy in His presence, content in His care, awed by His greatness, delighted by His surprises, secure in His love.

October 5

AWE-SOME *to* KNOW HIM

To You belongs silence
(the submissive wonder of reverence
which bursts forth into praise)
and praise is due and fitting to You,
O God, in Zion; and to You
shall the vow be performed.

PSALM 65:1 AMP

Walk in the wonder of the wondrous God. Live today in His amazing presence. Say in your heart, "There is no God like You." Go from faith to faith, and from wow to wow!

October 6

Your Comforter *and* Helper

The Helper, the Holy Spirit, whom the Father will send in My name, He will teach you all things, and bring to your remembrance all things that I said to you.

JOHN 14:26 NKJV

Father, thank You for the gift of the Holy Spirit. Jesus, thank You for sending the Holy Spirit to me. Holy Spirit, thank You for being my Comforter and my Helper. Thank You for Your presence and for caring about me. Thank You for the oil of joy that You pour into my heart. I know that Your oil is a healing joy. I welcome and receive today the healing and restoring power of Your joy.

October 7

He Comes *to* Us

A certain Samaritan, as he journeyed, came where he was. And when he saw him, he had compassion. So he went to him and bandaged his wounds, pouring on oil and wine; and he set him on his own animal, brought him to an inn, and took care of him.

LUKE 10:33–34 NKJV

The story of the Samaritan paints a compassionate picture of how Jesus comes to us in our times of greatest need. It is Jesus who cares for us and pours upon our wounds the oil of the Holy Spirit. Jesus has sent the Holy Spirit to be our Comforter and Helper.

Today, you can be assured that Jesus will not pass you by. He will come to you—to see to every detail, to pour out the oil of the Holy Spirit, and with His touch to bind up every wound.

October 8

God Uses You *to* Enrich Others

A word fitly spoken is like apples of gold in settings of silver.

PROVERBS 25:11 NKJV

Salt is a great benefit to society. It is one of the essential spices of life. For centuries salt has been highly prized, valued, and traded in the marketplace.

Saltiness helps to keep society's values strong, its laws just, and its honor strong.

In the grocery store you can now buy soda crackers that are salted on just one side. Jesus does not want you half-salted. Remain fully salted in the place God has you today. He wants you to speak, in season and out of season, the words He gives you to say.

October 9

Pure Words

The words of the Lord are pure words.

PSALM 12:6 KJV

Jeremiah said, *"Your words were found and I did eat them and Your word was to me the joy and the rejoicing of my heart."*

Peter told those who were babes in the Lord, *"Drink the sincere milk of the word."*

Jesus said, *"Live...on every word that proceeds from the mouth of God."*

The words the Lord speaks to you today are unadulterated, unmixed, and undefiled. His words are life and you can feast upon them with faith and heartfelt obedience.

October 10

Powerful Words

The word of the Lord holds true, and we can trust everything He does.

PSALM 33:4 NLT

God's words are:

Pure words, let them enrich you;

Clean words, let them wash you;

Holy words, let them sanctify you;

Wise words, let them instruct you;

Healthy words, let them feed you;

Powerful words, let them change you.

October 11

Sweet Words

They are more desirable than gold, even the finest gold. They are sweeter than honey, even honey dripping from the comb.

PSALM 19:10 NLT

God's words are:

True words, let them assure you;

Righteous words, let them guide you;

Healing words, let them strengthen you;

Tender words, let them comfort you;

Sure words, let them establish you;

Living words, let them nurture you;

Sweet words, let them delight you.

October 12

All Things Well

He has done all things well.

MARK 7:37 NKJV

A believer who had followed the Lord for many years made this simple but profound statement about Jesus: "Those dear feet have never mislead."

We can also add:

That assuring voice has never misspoken;

That gentle touch has never mistreated;

That faithful friendship has never betrayed;

That tender care has never abandoned;

That sweet fellowship has never disappointed;

That perfect love has never failed.

October 13

Contentment *in* Jesus (Part 1)

Now godliness with contentment is great gain.

I TIMOTHY 6:6 NKJV

His water quenches the thirsty;
There is no need to dig other wells.

His bread fills the hungry;
There is no need to gather crumbs.

His banqueting table is extravagant;
There is no need to go away empty.

His presence is fullness of joy;
There is no need to seek other ways to fulfillment.

October 14

Contentment *in* Jesus (Part 2)

Now godliness with contentment is great gain.

I TIMOTHY 6:6 NKJV

His will is perfect;

There is no need to acquire a better plan.

His wisdom is flawless;

There is no need to follow another point of view.

His grace is sufficient;

There is no need to obtain superficial help.

His redemption is complete;

There is no need to hunt for another savior.

His covenant is certain;

There is no need to trust a different guarantee.

October 15

Contentment *in* Jesus (Part 3)

Now godliness with contentment is great gain.
I TIMOTHY 6:6 NKJV

His kingdom is unshakable;
There is no need to find a more secure place.

His approval is enough;
There is no need to seek the applause of others.

His provision meets the need;
There is no need to worry.

His return is sure;
There is no need to let our hearts be troubled.

October 16

Perfect Peace

I will hear what God the Lord will speak,
for He will speak peace
to His people and to His saints.
PSALM 85:8 NKJV

Jesus whispers His peace to you. His whisper is the still small voice of the Holy Spirit. It is a peace that does not need to be loud to be heard. His peace runs deeper than any river. Trust in the Lord will always keep your heart and mind in the company of peace, rest, and hope.

October 17

Prayer *of* Help

The Lord is a warrior; Yahweh is His name!

EXODUS 15:3 NLT

Lord, I thank you that You are a Warrior and You never know defeat; You are a Conqueror and every enemy is under Your feet; You are a Deliverer and every foe will sound retreat.

I thank You, O God, that You preserve me. I take refuge in You and I am safe. I put my trust and confidence in You alone. I lean on You, for You will not falter or faint. You are my support and keep me from falling. You are my high tower and keep me from fleeing. You are my confidence and keep me from fearing.

October 18

Prayer *of* Protection *and* Victory

You are my Lord, my goodness is nothing apart from You.

PSALM 16:2 NKJV

Thank You, God, for being with me, beside me, behind me, and before me. You are always at my right hand and keep me secure. What joy it brings to know that when I call to You, You answer me. You are my perfect refuge from every storm and battle.

Thank You for being my sure place, and for providing me with the safe place under the shadow of Your wings. Lord, arise and rescue me from all evil, from every lie, and from every bondage. I stand upon You as my rock, I abide in You as my fortress. You are my covering. You are my shield. Thank You for saving me and for rescuing me from my enemies. You always hear my cry for help.

October 19

What God Wants You *to* See

This is eternal life, that they may know
You, the only true God, and Jesus
Christ whom You have sent.
JOHN 17:3 NKJV

In heartache, see the Healer.

In sorrow, see the Comforter.

In darkness, see the Light.

In suffering, see the Burden Bearer.

In discouragement, see the Lifter of your head.

In need, see the Intercessor.

In loneliness see the unfailing Friend.

October 20

Moments

My times are in your hand.
PSALM 31:15 ESV

In the prayerful moments—ask Him.
In the decision moments—follow Him.
In the lonely moments—know Him.
In the listening moments—hear Him.
In the unsure moments—believe Him.
In the active moments—serve Him.
In the waiting moments—trust Him.
In the hurting moments—touch Him.
For in all your moments, He is there
In goodness, in kindness, in love.

OCTOBER 21

HEART DESIRES FULFILLED

Trust in the LORD, and do good; dwell in the land, and feed on His faithfulness. Delight yourself also in the LORD, and He shall give you the desires of your heart. Commit your way to the LORD, trust also in Him, and He shall bring it to pass.... Rest in the LORD, and wait patiently for Him.

PSALM 37:3-5, 7 NKJV

"God carries in His heart the fulfillment to all the desires He has placed within yours." Author unknown

October 22

His Desires *in* Your Heart

God is working in you, giving you the desire and the power to do what pleases Him.
PHILIPPIANS 2:13 NLT

1. Ask God to place His desires in your heart.
2. He is the only One who can fulfill the desires He has placed within you—the fulfillment of these desires will glorify Him.
3. He places His desires in you as you delight in Him.
4. He wants you to trust in His faithfulness and power to fulfill those desires.
5. Wait for His time and never give up on any desire that God has placed within you.

October 23

As You Wait, Rest

For God alone my soul waits in silence and quietly submits to Him, For my hope is from Him.

PSALM 62:5 AMP

What should you do as you wait upon the Lord to fulfill the desires He has placed in your heart? Do not attempt to strive, manipulate, or struggle in yourself to fulfill them. God has promised you that *He will give you* the desires of your heart; God has said that *He will bring it to pass.*

As you wait, rest. Wait with a quiet heart. There is no benefit in pressing or pushing; be at peace knowing that God's purpose is good and His plan is always perfect.

October 24

The Solid Rock

The Lord is my rock, my fortress, and the One who rescues me; My God, my rock and strength in whom I trust and take refuge.

PSALM 18:2 AMP

The Lord is your *huge* Rock! Sometimes the storms of life or the darkness of circumstances can settle over your soul. In these times, you may wonder what has happened to the Rock you saw so vividly when things were clear and His presence was unobstructed. Be assured, He has not moved, changed, or disappeared. The darkness is temporary, the Rock is eternal. The storm will pass, the darkness will lift. Your Rock abides!

October 25

Your Life Is *in* His Hands

For You, O Lord, have made me glad
by Your works; At the works of
Your hands I joyfully sing.

PSALM 92:4 AMP

The best decision you ever made was to place your life into the hands of the One who made you—hands that work with SKILL; hands that guide with WISDOM; hands that shape with PURPOSE; hands that shelter with LOVE.

October 26

Your Life Is *in the* Best Hands

For You, Lord, have made me glad through Your work; I will triumph in the works of Your hands.

PSALM 92:4 NKJV

God's hands are:

More capable than a great surgeon;

More precise than a fine diamond cutter;

More creative than a master craftsman.

Your life is in His hands!

October 27

In Christ

How precious is Your lovingkindness, O God! Therefore the children of men put their trust under the shadow of Your wings. They are abundantly satisfied with the fullness of Your house, and You give them drink from the river of Your pleasures.

PSALM 36:7–8 NKJV

Because you are in Christ, you are a *partaker of His promises*. God welcomed you and brought you into His inheritance through grace the day you gave your heart to Him. You are in Christ, not separated from Him; you are a friend, not a stranger; you are an heir, not an alien; you are a child, not an orphan; you are in the household of faith, not an outsider looking in. He is your "yes" to every promise.

October 28

He Is *the* Seeking Shepherd

The Lord is my shepherd;
I shall not want.
PSALM 23:1 NKJV

To the lost sheep,
He is the seeking Shepherd.

To the needy sheep,
He is the providing Shepherd.

To the hurting sheep,
He is the comforting Shepherd.

To the bruised sheep,
He is the healing Shepherd.

To the anxious sheep,
He is the peaceful Shepherd.

October 29

He is *the* Protecting Shepherd

Lord, don't hold back Your tender mercies from me. Let Your unfailing love and faithfulness always protect me.

PSALM 40:11 NLT

To the wandering sheep,
He is the guiding Shepherd.

To the fearful sheep,
He is the protecting Shepherd.

To the lame sheep,
He is the carrying Shepherd.

To the discontented sheep,
He is the fulfilling Shepherd.

To the parched sheep,
He is the anointing Shepherd.

To the insecure sheep,
He is the reassuring Shepherd.

October 30

He Is *the* Merciful Shepherd

Hear me, O Lord; for Thy lovingkindness
is good: turn unto me according to the
multitude of Thy tender mercies.

PSALM 69:16 KJV

To the fallen sheep,
He is the merciful Shepherd.

To the nervous sheep,
He is the quieting Shepherd.

To the heavy laden sheep,
He is the restful Shepherd.

To the lonely sheep,
He is the ever-present Shepherd.

To the weary sheep,
He is the restoring Shepherd.

October 31

As Only Your Father Could

I will be a Father to you, and you shall be My sons and daughters, says the LORD *Almighty.*
II CORINTHIANS 6:18 NKJV

The things your sight does not observe
His eyes see clearly.
The things your thinking does not understand
His mind knows fully.
The things your hands cannot grasp
His hands hold firmly.
The things your strength cannot subdue
His power conquers completely.
The things your resources cannot fulfill
His riches meet abundantly.
The things your love cannot give
His heart gives endlessly!

November 1

Anxiety, Not Welcome

Anxiety in a man's heart weighs it down, But a good (encouraging) word makes it glad.

PROVERBS 12:25 AMP

Anxiety—don't carry it, walk with it, eat with it, live with it, or go to bed with it. Don't entertain it, support it, encourage it—not in big things or little things, present things or future things, pressing things or perplexing things. It is a foe not a friend, a downer not an edifier, a binder not a freer. It will quickly introduce you to its close cousins, fret and fear. When anxiety knocks at the door of your heart or mind, be sure to renounce it, reject it, and refuse it any place.

NOVEMBER 2

PRAY *about* EVERYTHING

Do not be anxious or worried about anything, but in everything [every circumstance and situation] by prayer and petition with thanksgiving, continue to make your [specific] requests known to God.

PHILIPPIANS 4:6 AMP

Instead of being anxious about anything, you can begin to pray about everything. You have a God to go to and talk to who hears and answers prayer. Mix your prayers with thankfulness. Thanksgiving reflects an attitude of gratefulness to God for inviting you to come to Him, and it shows that you truly trust Him to take care of you, regardless of your circumstances.

As you pray and trust God to work, He will give you the assurance that He is behind you, before you, and all around you. His assurance will be your peace. God doesn't give you circumstantial peace, but His peace, a peace that remains constant and undisturbed through every circumstance.

November 3

Peace Replaces Anxiety

And the peace of God [that peace which reassures the heart, that peace] which transcends all understanding, [that peace which] stands guard over your hearts and your minds in Christ Jesus [is yours].

PHILIPPIANS 4:7 AMP

God's peace is His answer for anxiety. His peace will quiet you and calm you; it will minister health to your nerves and rest to your spirit. God's peace is more powerful than anxiety, fear, or worry. God's peace strengthens you by giving you the assurance that God is for you and that no weapon formed against you will prosper.

November 4

Kept *by* His Peace

Lord, You will establish peace for us, Since You have also performed for us all that we have done.

ISAIAH 26:12 AMP

Never turn away from God's peace. Yield and surrender your heart and mind to His peace. Say, "Yes, Lord, I receive Your peace." You do not need to understand why certain things are happening in order to have God's peace. His peace transcends your understanding. God's peace is the peace that Jesus said He would give to you. It is a peace that the world cannot give you. His peace belongs to you because you belong to Him.

November 5

Nothing Is Too Hard *for the* Lord

Grace to you and peace [inner calm and spiritual well-being] from God our Father and from the Lord Jesus Christ.

ROMANS 1:7 AMP

Anxiety tells you that you are in a situation that is too big for God to handle;

Peace assures you that nothing is too hard for the Lord.

Anxiety assumes the worst will happen;

Peace affirms the best is yet to be.

Anxiety points you to your inadequacy;

Peace confirms that God's grace is sufficient.

Anxiety causes you to panic;

Peace causes you to be still.

Anxiety shows you your lack;

Peace points you to God's supply.

Anxiety warns of defeat and failure;

Peace proclaims God's victory and success.

November 6

Peace Is God's Pathway

Which of you by worrying can add one cubit to his stature? If you then are not able to do the least, why are you anxious for the rest?... But seek first the kingdom of God and His righteousness, and all these things shall be added to you.

LUKE 12:24–26, MATTHEW 6:33 NKJV

Anxiety causes you to strive;

Peace causes you to rest.

Anxiety says, "You will be carried away by the storm";

Peace says, "Your anchor holds."

Anxiety fills you with darkness;

Peace floods you with light.

Anxiety tells you to first seek a solution;

Peace tells you to first seek the Kingdom.

Anxiety tells you, "You won't make it";

Peace assures you, "God will bring you through."

November 7

Contentment

Now godliness with contentment is great gain.

I TIMOTHY 6:6 NKJV

At the heart of contentment is the assurance that God knows all about me, knows what is best for me, and is always doing the right thing concerning me.

November 8

Change

Now [in Haran] the Lord had said to Abram, "Go away from your country, and from your relatives and from your father's house, to the land which I will show you.... So Abram departed [in faithful obedience] as the Lord had directed him.

GENESIS 12:1, 4 AMP

Perhaps this is a time of change for you. If so, it will be a change based upon clear direction from the Lord. It is a step that will take you down a new pathway and away from the familiar, the convenient, or the comfortable. It is also, like Abram, a step that will open new adventures of faith. God will go before you and guide you to His appointed place.

November 9

Things Present, Things *to* Come

Therefore let no man glory in men. For all things are yours…things present, or things to come; all are yours; and ye are Christ's; and Christ is God's.

I CORINTHIANS 3:21–23 KJV

Some things are for now;

Some things are for later.

We need faith for what is now;

We need hope for what is later.

We need to be content for what is now;

We need to be patient for what is later.

November 10

Covered

You have hedged me behind and before, and laid Your hand upon me. Such knowledge is too wonderful for me; it is high, I cannot attain it.

PSALM 139:5–6 NKJV

Lord, thank You for Your hands of care and compassion. I know they are strong hands and mighty to save, to bless, to heal, to rescue, to deliver, and to make whole. Thank You that You will never let me go! As I follow You I know I will walk under the covering shadow of Your wings.

Thank You for every person who has been an extension of Your hand in my life. I ask You to cover them today, encourage them, and help them to know that You are using them for good in the lives of others. Use me today, Father, to be Your hand extended. Amen!

November 11

The One Who Believes

Now faith is the assurance (the confirmation, the title deed) of the things [we] hope for, being the proof of things [we] do not see and the conviction of their reality [faith perceiving as real fact what is not revealed to the senses].

HEBREWS 11:1 AMP

The one who believes God reigns can go through a day peacefully;

The one who believes God is holy can go through a day worshipfully;

The one who believes God is generous can go through a day thankfully;

The one who believes God is strong can go through a day joyfully;

The one who believes God is love can go through a day confidently;

The one who believes God is faithful can go through a day securely;

The one who believes God is victor can go through a day triumphantly.

November 12

Jesus, All *in* All

Christ is all that matters, and He lives in all of us.
COLOSSIANS 3:11 NLT

Jesus is not "part-time" in anything. He is not your some-in-some but your all-in-all; not your occasional help but your ever-present help in time of need; not the One who prays for you occasionally but the One who *ever lives* to make intercession for you.

Lord, the eyes of my faith look to You. I receive of Your limitless love, Your limitless grace, and Your limitless power. Jesus, be to me today all that You are, according to my need. Amen.

November 13

Things You Can Count On Now!

Therefore, we who have fled to Him for refuge can have great confidence as we hold to the hope that lies before us. This hope is a strong and trustworthy anchor for our souls.

HEBREWS 6:18–19 NLT

There is a grace that is sufficient; a mercy that endures; an atoning blood that cleanses; a hope that doesn't disappoint; a love that never fails; a purpose that works all things together for the good; a peace that passes understanding; a joy unspeakable; a kingdom unshakable; a foundation indestructible; a High Priest who prays; a Savior who lives; a Spirit who comforts; a Father who cares.

November 14

God Is *the* All-Sufficient One

Who is like You among the gods, O Lord?
Who is like You, majestic in holiness,
Awesome in splendor, working wonders?
EXODUS 15:11 AMP

God is all-wise and He does not pursue advice; God is all-powerful and He does not need aid; God is all-present and He does not seek information.

But God is holy and He does seek our worship; God is faithful and He does ask for our trust; God is love and He does call for our obedience.

November 15

The Measure (Part 1)

The Lord is my portion; I have promised to keep Your words.
PSALM 119:57 AMP

Let the grace of the Lord be the measure of your sufficiency; let the peace of the Lord be the measure of your quietness; let the power of the Lord be the measure of your strength; let the goodness of the Lord be the measure of your contentment; let the love of the Lord be the measure of your service.

November 16

The Measure (Part 2)

The poor shall eat and be satisfied; those who seek Him will praise the Lord. Let your heart live forever!

PSALM 22:26 NKJV

Let the faithfulness of the Lord be the measure of your trust; let the beauty of the Lord be the measure of your worship; let the fullness of the Lord be the measure of your joy; let the sovereignty of the Lord be the measure of your confidence; let the promises of the Lord be the measure of your expectations; let the coming of the Lord be the measure of hope.

November 17

Jesus, Altogether Wonderful

And He will be called: Wonderful Counselor.

ISAIAH 9:6 NLT

Your peace? Jesus gives it. Your purpose? Jesus defines it. Your future? Jesus holds it. Your soul? Jesus restores it. Your strength? Jesus renews it. Your life? Jesus sustains it. Your walk? Jesus directs it. Your service? Jesus anoints it. Your sufficiency? Jesus maintains it. Your fruitfulness? Jesus multiplies it. Your day? Jesus blesses it. Your hope? Jesus secures it. Your home in heaven? Jesus prepares it.

November 18

Jesus, Altogether Mighty

And He will be called…Mighty God.

ISAIAH 9:6 NLT

Your good? Jesus wills it.

Your redemption? Jesus bought it.

Your hand? Jesus holds it.

Your pathway? Jesus walks it.

Your destiny? Jesus secures it.

Your ministry? Jesus ordains it.

Your place? Jesus establishes it.

Your wisdom? Jesus speaks it.

Your anxiety? Jesus quiets it.

Your worship? Jesus receives it.

Your heart? Jesus knows it.

November 19

Prayer of Service

But whatever I am now, it is all because God poured out His special favor on me.... It was not I but God who was working through me by His grace.

I CORINTHIANS 15:10 NLT

Jesus, use my voice to speak as You spoke; use my ears to listen as You listened; use my hands to bless as You blessed; use my feet to walk as You walked; use my life to serve as You served; use my heart to love as You loved.

November 20

Magnify *the* Lord

O magnify the Lord with me, and let us exalt His name together.

PSALM 34:3 KJV

It is only through brokenness, humility, and repentance that we can fully magnify who the Lord is and what He has done in our lives. For it is out of our poverty that we magnify His riches; out of our smallness that we magnify His greatness; out of our frailty that we magnify His power; out of our need that we magnify His fullness; out of our deficiency that we magnify His abundance; out of our unworthiness that we magnify His mercies; out of our weakness that we magnify His strength; out of our insufficiency that we magnify His grace.

November 21

The Name *of the* Lord

We will trust in and boast of the name of the Lord our God.

PSALM 20:7 AMP

His name—mighty, magnificent, majestic. You can call upon the name of the Lord at any time, in any circumstance, for any reason. It is a good thing, the right thing, and the wise thing to call upon the name of the Lord. There is no name like His name—no other title is so splendid, no other declaration is so honorable, no other proclamation is so glorious, no other person is so praiseworthy!

November 22

Call upon *the* Name *of the* Lord

Oh, give thanks to the Lord! Call upon His name; make known His deeds among the peoples!

I Chronicles 16:8 NKJV

You call upon the name of the Lord in prayer and petition, in supplication and intercession, in praise and thanksgiving. You call upon His name because He hears your call and listens to your cry, because He understands and cares about your situation, because He has all power to answer and work in your behalf.

In the name of the Lord you can speak with conviction, act with boldness, live with confidence, walk with clarity, and minister with authority.

The name of the Lord is completely dependable and reliable—in His name you put your trust, set up your banner, sing your praise, find your courage, take your stand, move forward, and overcome.

November 23

He Has a Name for Every Need

I will protect those who trust in My name.

PSALM 91:14 NLT

I believe in His name "Righteousness" (Jeremiah 23:6). His righteousness clothes me with the robe of purity.

I believe in His name "There" (Ezekiel 48:35). He is the One who is always with me, in every moment, through every circumstance.

I believe in His name "Peace" (Judges 6:24). In Him I find my rest, my calm assurance, my shalom.

I believe in His name "Banner" (Exodus 17:15). He is my Victor, Champion, Captain, King. He is my Warrior and the victor in every battle.

I believe in His name "Will See, Will Provide" (Genesis 22:14). He is in the details of life, is before me, and supplies every need.

November 24

Blessed Be *the* Name *of the* Lord

Blessed be the name of the Lord from this time forth and for evermore.
PSALM 113:2 KJV

I believe in His name "Healer" (Exodus 15:26). He is my Physician, my Comforter, my health, my wholeness, and my restorer.

I believe in His name "Sanctifier" (Exodus 31:13). He sets me aside for His purposes, cleanses my heart, and washes me with His Word.

I believe in His name "Shepherd" (Psalm 23:1). He leads me, feeds me, guides me, and will not fail me, leave me, or forsake me.

I believe in His name "Maker, Creator" (Psalm 95:6). He formed me with His hands, brought me into this world for a purpose, keeps me in His care, and is shaping me into His image.

NOVEMBER 25

THE BLESSING *of* SHALOM

Then Gideon built an altar there unto the LORD, and called it Jehovahshalom.
JUDGES 6:24 KJV

The word "shalom" has many significant meanings throughout the Scriptures. The following blessing is a compilation of those meanings.

May you be whole in body, soul, and spirit as a result of being in harmony with God's will and purpose for your life.

May His peace be your covering, your heart know His fullness, and by His mighty power may you know victory over every enemy.

May you know the healing power of His presence and the restoration of every broken relationship.

Through His sufficiency, may every need that you face be met by His limitless resources.

May His covenant promises be fulfilled in your life and in your family.

May He bring you the greatest measure of contentment and the deepest satisfaction that your heart can possibly know.

November 26

Faith

Therein is the righteousness of God revealed from faith to faith: as it is written, The just shall live by faith.

ROMANS 1:17 KJV

Faith sees what your physical eyes can never see.

Faith knows what your natural mind can never comprehend.

Faith possesses what your physical arms can never hold.

Faith says yes to everything God declares to be true.

Faith stands upon everything God says is certain, it leans upon everything God says is unmovable, and it counts upon everything God says will come to pass.

NOVEMBER 27

THE SHEPHERD'S WAYS

The LORD is my shepherd; I shall not want.

PSALM 23:1 KJV

He doesn't drive, He leads.
He doesn't deplete, He feeds.
He doesn't withdraw, He resides.
He doesn't flee, He abides.
He doesn't shun, He confides.
He doesn't withhold, He provides.
He doesn't misuse, He affirms.
He doesn't confuse, He confirms.
He doesn't provoke, He consoles.
He doesn't ignore, He upholds.
He doesn't avoid, He feels.
He doesn't mistreat, He heals.
He doesn't retreat, He pursues.
He doesn't quench, He renews.
He doesn't drain, He fills.
He doesn't trouble, He stills.

November 28

What Can't Be Taken Away

I am convinced and confident of this very thing, that He who has begun a good work in you will [continue to] perfect and complete it until the day of Christ Jesus [the time of His return].

PHILIPPIANS 1:6 AMP

All that you have comes from God and is maintained by Him.

What is maintained by Him is also sustained by Him.

It is also increased by Him so that you can grow from strength to strength and from glory to glory.

NOVEMBER 29

ALL *in* ALL

Christ is all and in all.

COLOSSIANS 3:11 NKJV

Your bondages? Jesus breaks them. Your enemies? Jesus conquers them. Your diseases? Jesus heals them. Your transgressions? Jesus removes them. Your fears? Jesus overcomes them. Your burdens? Jesus carries them. Your sins? Jesus cleanses them. Your storms? Jesus stills them. Your sorrows? Jesus comforts them. Your pains? Jesus soothes them. Your worries? Jesus dispels them. Your longings? Jesus fulfills them. Your needs? Jesus meets them.

November 30

Preparation

The Lord directs the steps of the godly. He delights in every detail of their lives.

PSALM 37:23 NLT

As you prepare to enter into the busy days of December, keep these five things in mind:

Place—Be in God's appointed place.

Purpose—Believe God's purpose for you will be fulfilled in the place He has you.

Plan—Have confidence that nothing can frustrate God's perfect plan for you.

Power—Receive His Spirit to equip and empower you to do what He has called you to do.

Peace—Let His peace keep you at rest in the place He has called you.

December 1

Three Things I Believe

Whom having not seen you love. Though now you do not see Him, yet believing, you rejoice with joy inexpressible and full of glory.

I PETER 1:8 NKJV

1. **I believe in what Jesus has said.** I cannot know what Jesus has said without knowing the Scriptures. His words are true words, good words, living words, whole words, righteous words.

2. **I believe in what God can do.** I do not place any limits upon God. I believe my life is in His hands and He is taking care of me.

3. **I believe in the Holy Spirit's leading.** The Holy Spirit is in me and will guide me into all truth. He always knows what He is doing.

December 2

I Believe God Loves Me

We love because he first loved us.

I JOHN 4:19 ESV

I believe God loves me consistently, faithfully, righteously. He loves me to the height, to the breadth and length and depth of His being. His love sought me, wooed me, received me, embraced me, adopted me, brought me into His family, and made me His child and heir.

I believe His love assures me of His acceptance, extends to me His mercies, and covers me with His grace.

The signature of His love is written over my life—it feeds me in my hunger, upholds me in my trials, and heals me in my pain. It bathes me with comfort, soothes me with oil, and clothes me with kindness. It protects me in the battle, holds me in the storm, guides me in the journey, and keeps me to the end.

December 3

You Belong *to* God

Do you not know that your body is the temple (the very sanctuary) of the Holy Spirit Who lives within you, Whom you have received [as a Gift] from God? You are not your own, you were bought with a price [purchased with a preciousness and paid for, made His own]. So then, honor God and bring glory to Him in your body.

I CORINTHIANS 6:19–20 AMP

God's ownership of your life brings great comfort, deep peace, and overflowing joy. His ownership means that you are in His hands, in His care, in His keeping. As your Redeemer He has taken full responsibility for your life because He has purchased it.

The hands of your Redeemer are strong hands, creative hands, caring hands, giving hands, healing hands, keeping hands. Today your life is in His hands—to do His will, to gladden His heart, to praise His name.

December 4

See Jesus

Sir, we would see Jesus.

JOHN 12:21 KJV

The right focus of your faith will bring Jesus into clear view. To focus on Jesus means to be taken up with Him, to put Him at the center, to listen to what He says, and to see life from His perspective.

You need to turn your eyes away from everything, anything, or anyone that distracts you from seeing Jesus. As you see Jesus, your faith will not be focused on your past sins but on the Savior; not on your past failures but on the Victor; not on your past hurts but on the Healer.

As you see Jesus, your faith will not be focused on your present weaknesses but on the Almighty One; not on your present anxieties but on the Prince of Peace; not on your problems but on the All-Sufficient One.

December 5

Prayer to See Jesus

You are worthy, O Lord our God, to receive glory and honor and power.
REVELATION 4:11 NLT

Jesus, I want to see You, for no other face can show me the Father, and no other light can reveal His image. I want to know what it fully means to have the eyes of my heart opened to behold the beauty of the Lord, and to be in awe of Your glory. Reveal to me the grace upon Your countenance, the joy within Your spirit, and the love that moves Your heart toward mine.

Jesus, I wait upon You, come to me; I listen for You, speak to me; I look to You, show me; I lean on You, keep me. I thank You for being the hope of my heart, the joy of my life, and the reason I live.

December 6

As He Works *in* You...

God is working in you, giving you the desire and the power to do what pleases Him.
PHILIPPIANS 2:13 NLT

Step out in faithful obedience;

Reach out to touch others;

Give out as freely as He has given to you;

Move out with grace and compassion;

Speak out His words of life and hope;

Live out what He is working within;

Pour out praise from a grateful heart.

December 7

Hands *to* Serve

You go before me and follow me. You place Your hand of blessing on my head.

PSALM 139:5 NLT

God will work through your hands,

To support someone who is weak,

To raise someone who has fallen,

To uphold someone who is weary,

To wipe a tear,

To hold a hand,

To give a cup of water,

To share a burden,

To impart a blessing.

December 8

The Song *of* Healing

The Lord is my strength and my song; He has given me victory.
PSALM 118:14 NLT

Father, You're the strength that lifts the burden,

You're the oil that soothes the pain;

You're the sunlight when there's darkness,

You're the shelter in the rain.

You're the hand that brings all healing,

You're the song that calms all fear;

You're the peace that brings all comfort,

You're the God who's always near.

December 9

Faithful

O Lord God of Heaven's Armies!
Where is there anyone as mighty as You,
O Lord? You are entirely faithful.

PSALM 89:8 NLT

The God you trusted in the past is the One who's faithful still.

Trust Him now, with all your heart, to be working out His will.

There's nothing that you're facing that takes Him by surprise.

All the things concerning you have not escaped His eyes.

His grace has been your covering through every circumstance.

Everything will work for good; nothing is by chance.

Let your faith abide in Him just like a mustard seed,

And you will find His promise true to meet your every need.

December 10

Be *at* Peace (Part 1)

Be anxious for nothing, but in everything....
PHILIPPIANS 4:6 NKJV

Be anxious for nothing... Never allow or carry about with you an anxious thought or make it a part of your day or your life. Not one thing should be allowed to move you into a state of anxiety or fret.

but (always)... At any time, at any place, and in every circumstance there is another option provided for you.

in everything... Nothing needs to be left out; every detail of your life is included and is important to God because He cares about you.

December 11

Be *at* Peace (Part 2)

Be anxious for nothing, but in everything by prayer and supplication, with thanksgiving, let your requests be made known to God....

PHILIPPIANS 4:6 NKJV

By prayer... As an expression of worship; speaking directly to God (you praying, not someone in your behalf); not wishes, luck, or tossing coins in a fountain.

and supplication... Praying specifically, not in generalities.

with thanksgiving... With a right attitude of heart, appreciative of who God is and grateful for what He has done.

let your requests be made known to God... Don't just think about it but actually do it.

God hears your requests and He will answer.

December 12

Be *at* Peace (Part 3)

Be anxious for nothing, but in everything by prayer and supplication, with thanksgiving, let your requests be made known to God; and the peace of God, which surpasses all understanding, will guard your hearts and minds through Christ Jesus.

PHILIPPIANS 4:6–7 NKJV

And the peace of God... Not the peace of man, or circumstances. God never loses His peace.

which surpasses all understanding... Your peace is not based on whether you can understand how God is going to work things out.

will guard your hearts and minds... His peace is the sentinel who will stand guard as a defensive force to protect you from the spirit of fear.

through Christ Jesus... The Prince of Peace...not through any other name, religion, or resource. Not through our good deeds or good moods. Jesus is and will always be our only option, our only way, our only hope.

December 13

Confidence *in* Prayer

Let us therefore come boldly to the throne of grace, that we may obtain mercy and find grace to help in time of need.
HEBREWS 4:16 NKJV

Let us... No one needs to be left out, the invitation is to all.

therefore come boldly... Come with complete confidence and without fear of rejection.

to the throne of grace... Be specific regarding where you are and who you are speaking to. The throne is the place of absolute authority; no one else can overrule Him. Grace makes prayer possible, not your performance.

that we may obtain mercy... Mercy means access, not judgment. The blood is on the mercy seat and that is the basis of coming, asking, and receiving.

and find grace to help in time of need... Your needy time is your time for prayer. Help is on the way... the right help, adequate help, help at exactly the right time.

December 14

Love Sent Jesus

For God loved the world so much that He gave His one and only Son, so that everyone who believes in Him will not perish but have eternal life.

JOHN 3:16 NLT

Everything that is true proclaims God loves us—His Word tells us, Jesus' birth tells us, the cross tells us, the resurrection tells us, the Holy Spirit tells us. God's every action demonstrates His love, His every attribute confirms His love, His every attitude reveals His love. Jesus is God's gift of love, perfectly given for us to welcome, to believe, and to receive.

December 15

Unfailing Love

Love never fails.

I CORINTHIANS 13:8 NKJV

God's love will never fail us, never disappoint us, never let us down, nor ever let us go. He loves us patiently, perfectly, practically, protectively, purely. His love will never give up on us, and will endure through every circumstance.

God's love seeks what is the highest, the richest, the fullest, and the best. All that His heart desires for us can only be found in His Son. It is only in Jesus' love that we are fulfilled, satisfied, joyful, peaceful, and complete.

December 16

Jesus Is Holy Light

In Him was life, and the life was the light of men.
JOHN 1:4 NKJV

Jesus is pure light, clean light, holy light. He is pure without spot, blemish, or stain. His motives are pure, causing us to welcome His ways; His thoughts are pure, causing us to seek His mind; His will is pure, causing us to follow His steps.

The light that shines from His heart to ours is free of anything that would contaminate our souls. Jesus is wholly beautiful and beautifully holy—lovely to look upon, worthy to call upon.

He is the majesty of all that is majestic, the splendor of all that is splendid. Jesus is the grandest of all that is grand, the highest of all that is high, the mightiest of all that is mighty. He is truly the altogether lovely One, the One our hearts can freely worship.

December 17

Savior from Sin

She will bring forth a Son, and you shall call His name JESUS, for He will save His people from their sins.

MATTHEW 1:21 NKJV

When our sins are forgiven it means that we have been justified. Justified means that we are set free from the guilt of all our past sins. How good, and kind, and gracious God has been to us! Through the blood of Jesus Christ He has set us free from the burden of our sins, He has washed us from the stain of our sins, He has redeemed us from the enslavement of our sins, He has healed us from the pain of our sins, He has comforted us from the sorrow of our sins, He has lifted us from the weight of our sins, and He has pardoned us from the judgment of our sins. A heart that is forgiven is a happy heart.

December 18

Messiah, Savior (Part 1)

O Lord, if You heal me, I will be truly healed; if You save me, I will be truly saved. My praises are for You alone!

JEREMIAH 17:14 NLT

Scripture promised Him. Genesis 3:15

Abraham believed in Him. Galatians 3:6–8,16–18

Moses lived for Him. Hebrews 11:23–26

Isaiah prophesied about Him. Isaiah 53

David knew of Him. Mark 12:35–36

Israel hoped for Him. Jeremiah 17:13–14

Elizabeth blessed Him. Luke 1:43

Mary magnified Him. Luke 1:46–47

Shepherds spoke of Him. Luke 2:17–18

Wise men worshipped Him. Matthew 2:11

December 19

Messiah, Savior (Part 2)

Therefore, God elevated Him to the place of highest honor and gave Him the name above all other names, that at the name of Jesus every knee should bow, in heaven and on earth and under the earth, and every tongue declare that Jesus Christ is Lord, to the glory of God the Father.

PHILIPPIANS 2:9–11 NLT

Simeon looked upon Him. Luke 2:25–30

Anna testified of Him. Luke 2:36-38

John wrote of Him. John 20:31

God anointed Him. Acts 10:38

Disciples walked with Him. Matthew 4:19

Seekers talked with Him. Luke 24:32

Thomas confessed Him. John 20:28

Peter proclaimed Him. Acts 2:22–36

Paul lived for Him. Philippians 1:21

Believers received Him. John 1:12

All will acknowledge Him, Jesus Christ the Lord. Philippians 2:9–11

DECEMBER 20

THERE IS *a* LOVE

Christ will make His home in your hearts as you trust in Him. Your roots will grow down into God's love and keep you strong. And may you have the power to understand, as all God's people should, how wide, how long, how high, and how deep His love is. May you experience the love of Christ, though it is too great to understand fully. Then you will be made complete with all the fullness of life and power that comes from God.

EPHESIANS 3:17–19 NLT

Oh, the love that has been given you—

A Child born, a Son given!

A love…

Extending to the breadth,

Descending to the depths,

Ascending to the heights,

Transcending all the places your heart can go.

December 21

Jesus *among* Us

The Word became flesh and dwelt among us,
and we beheld His glory, the glory as of the only
begotten of the Father, full of grace and truth.
JOHN 1:14 NKJV

Jesus was the Word made flesh who lived among us—it was His hands, His voice, His face that revealed the Father's glory! It was Jesus' hands that lifted the weary, His voice that spoke peace to the fearful, His face that looked upon the needy with compassion. It is His hand that now upholds you, His voice that now nurtures you, His face that now shines upon you.

December 22

Savior

There is born to you this day in the city of David a Savior, who is Christ the Lord.

LUKE 2:10–11 NKJV

"Savior" is Jesus' glorious name! It was spoken by heaven's angels to the shepherds who watched over their flocks by night. Jesus is the light of your salvation. His light brought you out of darkness and filled your heart with the joy of His salvation.

The day you received Jesus was the day you received the Father's perfect gift! Oh, what gladness and celebration came to God's heart on that day!

December 23

Precious Name *of* Jesus

Unto us a Child is born, unto us a Son is given;
and the government will be upon His shoulder.
And His name will be called Wonderful, Counselor,
Mighty God, Everlasting Father, Prince of Peace.

ISAIAH 9:6 NKJV

The prophets revealed many of Jesus' names. They did this so you could know what He wants to be to you throughout your life.

"Shepherd" is one of His most endearing names. As your Shepherd, He is leading you. Feeding you. Sheltering you. Protecting you.

"Prince of Peace" is a name spoken by the prophet Isaiah. Peace is not something Jesus has, it is who He is. You have peace today because you have Him.

"Mighty God" is another name spoken by the prophet Isaiah. He has not come to be your best option but your only option. He has the power to be that to you every day.

December 24

His Way *with* Us

Of the increase of His government and peace there will be no end, upon the throne of David and over His kingdom, to order it and establish it with judgment and justice from that time forward, even forever. The zeal of the LORD of hosts will perform this.

ISAIAH 9:7 NKJV

Jesus came in a way that fulfilled so much;
Spoke in a way that taught so much;
Lived in a way that revealed so much;
Blessed in a way that gave so much;
Died in a way that provided so much;
Arose in a way that conquered so much;
Loved in a way that meant so much.

December 25

Into *the* World Came

Behold, a virgin shall be with child, and shall bring forth a son, and they shall call His name Emmanuel, which being interpreted is, God with us.
MATTHEW 1:23 KJV

Into the world came…

God's purest Light to show us the way;

God's perfect Savior to free us from sin;

God's tender Shepherd to care for our needs;

God's sure Foundation to make us secure;

God's fullest Joy to give us a new song;

God's broken Bread to satisfy our hunger;

God's conquering King to rule in our hearts;

God's healing Fountain to make us whole;

God's quieting Peace to bring us rest;

God's redeeming Love to make us His own.

December 26

The Gift

When they had come into the house, they saw the young Child with Mary His mother, and fell down and worshiped Him.

MATTHEW 2:11 NKJV

May the following prayer draw you closer to the One who is the Gift too wonderful for words.

Lord Jesus, I open my heart to You. You are the One who came for me, died for me, and rose for me. You are my Savior! Thank You for being present in my life as my Daily Bread, my Living Water, my Word of Life, my Prince of Peace, and my Song of Songs. In darkness I receive Your light, in weakness I receive Your strength, and in hard times I receive Your overcoming grace. Thank You for being the Way that leads me to the Father's heart, and for being the Life that can never be depleted or taken away. Amen!

December 27

God Is True

The Lord is the true God and
the God who is Truth.
JEREMIAH 10:10 AMP

God is the true God. From Him, and Him alone, comes all truth. He is true in His character and nature. He will never speak a lie or deceive you in any way. He is true to you. God is your true north, your anchor point, and your confidence. You can walk ahead in the coming year with your eyes set upon Him, your faith resting in Him, and your heart fixed upon Him.

December 28

The Invitation

Come to me, all of you who are weary and carry heavy burdens, and I will give you rest. Take My yoke upon you. Let Me teach you, because I am humble and gentle at heart, and you will find rest for your souls. For My yoke is easy to bear, and the burden I give you is light.

MATTHEW 11:28–30 NLT

The Invitation: Come

The Destination: to Me

The Qualification: all you who labor and are heavy laden

The Consolation: and I will give you rest.

The Identification: Take My yoke upon you and learn from Me,

The Disposition: for I am gentle and lowly in heart,

The Impartation: and you will find rest for your souls.

The Liberation: For My yoke is easy and My burden is light.

December 29

In God's Hands

Fear not, for I am with you; be not dismayed,
for I am your God. I will strengthen
you, yes, I will help you, I will uphold
you with My righteous right hand.

ISAIAH 41:10 NKJV

Today is in God's hands, and so are you.
His hands are strong and will uphold you;
His hands are great and will enfold you;
His hands are gentle and will embrace you;
His hands are protective and will cover you;
His hands are reassuring and will quiet you;
His hands are powerful and will defend you;
His hands are masterful and will conform you;
His hands are compassionate and will care for you;
His hands are healing and will renew you;
His hands are calming and will comfort you;
His hands are giving and will bless you.

December 30

Let God Choose

As for God, His way is perfect.
PSALM 18:30 NKJV

As you approach the coming year, let God choose for you...

Let God plan for you, it will be the right timing.

Let God measure for you, it will be the right portion.

Let God help you, it will be the right care.

Let God instruct you, it will be the right teaching.

Let God prepare you, it will be the right training.

Let God counsel you, it will be the right perspective.

Let God fight for you, it will be the right outcome.

Let God work in you, it will be the right result.

December 31

Countdown—Ten Kingdom Certainties *for the* New Year

I have loved you with an everlasting love.

JEREMIAH 31:3 NKJV

10. God remains, as He always has, upon His throne. Psalm 47:8
9. His grace will continue to abound. Romans 5:20
8. His mercies will always be new every morning. Lamentations 3:22
7. His promises will always be true and yes in Jesus. II Corinthians 1:20
6. He will remain faithful. Isaiah 49:7
5. He will continue working out His plan. Ephesians 1:11
4. He will never fail to provide. Philippians 4:19
3. He will daily bless you with every spiritual blessing in Christ. Ephesians 1:3
2. His blood will always have the power to cleanse you from all sin. I John 1:7
1. His love for you will never know a day of failure. Jeremiah 31:3

May the Lord bless and enrich your life daily as you take your place at His table in the coming year

Dear Friend,

This book was prayerfully crafted with you, the reader, in mind—every word, every sentence, every page—was thoughtfully written, designed, and packaged to encourage you...right where you are this very moment. At DaySpring, our vision is to see every person experience the life-changing message of God's love. So, as we worked through rough drafts, design changes, edits and details, we prayed for you to deeply experience His unfailing love, indescribable peace, and pure joy. It is our sincere hope that through these Truth-filled pages your heart will be blessed, knowing that God cares about you—your desires and disappointments, your challenges and dreams.

He knows. He cares. He loves you unconditionally.

BLESSINGS!
THE DAYSPRING BOOK TEAM